the SOUL *of the*
CHILD

Previous Books by Michael Gurian

Parenting
The Wonder of Girls
The Wonder of Boys
A Fine Young Man
The Good Son
What Stories Does My Son Need?
(with Terry Trueman)

Education
Boys and Girls Learn Differently!
(with Patricia Henley and Terry Trueman)

Psychology
Love's Journey
Mothers, Sons and Lovers
The Prince and the King

For Young Adults
Understanding Guys
From Boys to Men

Fiction and Poetry
An American Mystic
The Odyssey of Telemachus
Emptying

the SOUL of the CHILD

Nurturing the Divine Identity of Our Children

MICHAEL GURIAN

ATRIA BOOKS

New York London Toronto Sydney Singapore

ATRIA BOOKS

1230 Avenue of the Americas
New York, NY 10020

ISBN 13: 978-1-4165-7041-7   ISBN 10: 1-4165-7041-1

First Atria Books hardcover printing November 2002

10 9 8 7 6 5 4 3 2 1

ATRIA BOOKS is a trademark of Simon & Schuster, Inc.

For information regarding special discounts for bulk purchases,
please contact Simon & Schuster Special Sales at 1-800-456-6798
or business@simonandschuster.com

Printed in the U.S.A

For Gabrielle and Davita

ACKNOWLEDGMENTS

Special thanks are due my wife, Gail, who supports me as I explore the fields of science, religion, and child development. I have been lucky to have her as a friend, partner, and teacher.

Profound thanks are also due to my children, Gabrielle and Davita, who have given me purpose and challenged my mind and heart to discover the deep, hidden places of human experience.

No book can reach its audience without the graceful work of editor, publisher, and agent. Tracy Behar, my editor, has blessed this project from the very beginning with her vision and support. Special thanks are also due to Judith Curr, my publisher, who has been a passionate advocate of this project. Brenda Copeland has been a gracious friend throughout the process of publication, following up on all the important details and providing her own wealth of vision. Thanks are also due to the publicity staff at Atria Books, as well as to so many others behind the scenes.

Candice Fuhrman and Alan Rinzler were instrumental in making sure this book found a home and developed a future. Many thanks to them for their wisdom and direction.

This project has had many other friends, too numerous to name, who have inspired me by devoting their lives to the care of children. May they feel supported as they do the hard work of tending the light.

CONTENTS

Introduction   xv

     A Vision   *xxi*

     The Book   *xxii*

     The New Human   *xxv*

PART I: THE SOUL OF THE CHILD

Chapter 1. The Science of the Soul:

     Proof of the Soul's Existence   3

     The Monitors   *5*

     Thinking Differently about the Science of the Soul   *7*

     Seeing the Light   *9*

     The Science of the Soul   *19*

     The Soul Right Before Our Eyes   *26*

     Beyond the Soul/Body Split   *32*

     Where We Go from Here   *35*

Chapter 2. The Soul Grows:

     Soul Development from Birth to Adulthood   39

     Watch the Light Grow   *42*

     The Secret Life of a Child   *43*

     The Human Journey of Individualization   *45*

The Science of Soul Growth   50

Flowering   58

Soul Growth, Stress, and Cortisol   61

Protecting the Light   65

The Precious Child   67

Chapter 3. Soul Markings:

      The Divine Map a Child Is Born With   69

The Divine Child   76

Genetics: Soul Markings   80

Does Your Child Have a Destiny?   84

What Is Evil?   95

What Is Death?   104

PART II: GOD IS THE CHILD

Chapter 4. The New Human:

      How Our Thinking Must Change   115

Unifying the Field   118

The New Human   122

The Future of Religion   126

Bridging the Gap between Soul and Body   137

The Future of the Child   139

Chapter 5. Soul Retrieval:

      The Personal Journey Back to the Soul   145

The Science of Lost Soul   148

The Science of Soul Retrieval   153

The New Human: Putting Children First   165

Chapter 6. God Is the Child:

     The Future of the Family   169

God Needs Us   174

The Loneliness of the Child   179

The Future of the Family   185

The Family of the Future   191

When God Is the Child   196

Moving Beyond Individualism   198

Epilogue   201

Notes and References   203

Books That Help Nurture the Soul of the Child   211

About the Author   215

Index   217

The highest measure of a civilization lies in how it cares for its children.

—Margaret Mead

INTRODUCTION

The greatest tragedy in human life is to live
unaware of one's divine identity.

—REVEREND WILLIAM HARPER HOUFF

Blair is a small town about an hour from Omaha, set into
the green fields, low hills, and open plains of eastern
Nebraska. Most of the people who live in Blair also work there,
as farmers, schoolteachers, or shopkeepers. A few commute to a
larger city or neighboring town for employment or travel to visit
family.

My children's great-grandmother, Laura, a woman of ninety-
five, lives in Blair at a nursing home. She has accomplished much in
her long life, including raising three children with her husband and
then without him, helping to run a chicken farm, and teaching elementary school. She is my children's oldest living relative.

She is also very frail, thinks of herself not only as living but also
as dying. "It is time for my soul to leave my body," she said once.
Neither her vision nor her balance is good. She can no longer live

independently and now exists in that time of life between life and death, and has the wisdom to know it.

Once while visiting her, my daughters and I took a walk on the parklike grounds of the nursing home, which sat near the edge of town. We had just come downstairs—the children and I needed a little time walking outdoors after spending an hour in Laura's small room. The three of us were saddened, as we walked, by how quickly Great-grandma's soul did seem to be leaving her body—almost like air gradually leaking out of a balloon. Her body's skin was shriveling and pale, her presence in the teaming, vital world contracting before our eyes—and yet we also simultaneously experienced a different emotion that was difficult to describe, almost a mysterious sense of anticipation. We knew something incredible awaited Great-grandma, though we didn't know what it was.

Davita, who was eight, asked me, "Where will Great-grandma's body go when she dies?"

"Probably into the ground," I replied.

"What about her soul?"

Though tempted, as most parents are, to say "heaven" when a small child inquires about death, I said instead, "We don't know for sure. We could say she's going to heaven. We could say she's returning to nature itself, to the trees and the wheat fields out there." I pointed to the green plain at the horizon that surrounds Blair, Nebraska.

"Her soul will be out there, all around?" Davita asked.

"Maybe." I smiled. "We don't exactly know what happens to the soul after death."

Gabrielle, almost twelve, had been chewing on the moist end of a long blade of grass. Now she entered the conversation.

"Dad," she said, "what is the soul made of?" She had been to Christian and Jewish Sunday schools over the years. My wife, Gail, is of Nebraskan Protestant stock; I am of New York Jewish origin; our daughters have thus heard both Christian and Jewish answers to questions about the soul. Because we have lived overseas and are interested in world religions, they've heard Hindu, Buddhist, Muslim, and other responses as well. Yet I don't think she had ever heard an answer to this specific question. It was a somewhat unusual one: what *material* is the human soul composed of?

My instantaneous answer was to stall. "What do you mean?" I asked.

She thought for a moment. "What's a soul made of?" She did her best to ask again a question that I had no answer to at that moment.

I responded honestly, "I don't really know. I'm not sure anybody does."

"Well, but I know," she said.

I raised my eyebrows, amused. "Really?"

"Yes. It's made of God."

"The soul is made of God," I repeated back to her. "Okay. And what is God made of?"

She frowned. Behind her eyes her mind whirred, trying to figure out the logical quandary she'd walked right into.

"I guess I can't say 'God is made of the soul,' can I?" she thought aloud, applying simple logic.

"You could actually," I said, "and you're most certainly right. But it wouldn't answer your question the way you want it answered, would it?"

"No," she agreed.

"When Great-grandma dies," Davita said, interrupting our

intellectual discourse, "will all the lights go out in her soul?"

"I don't know for sure," I responded. "But every wise teacher from all over the world seems to agree that her body will become dark when her soul leaves."

"That's what her soul is made of, then," Gabrielle said triumphantly. "It's made of light."

"Light?"

"Yes. Light." Gabrielle, still a little girl at eleven, yet beginning to develop the mind of an adult, looked at me with certainty. And now, I must admit, behind my own eyes, my mind began to whirr at a fast rate. Thoughts from the Bhagavad Gita, the Sutras, the Old Testament, the New Testament, the Koran, flew into my mind. "Be ye lamps upon the world." "You are light for all the world." "Light particles are energy—they cannot be destroyed." "The brain on a PET scan shows life because it lights up." Pieces of Newtonian and quantum physics, like children's rhymes, replayed themselves in my mind. Einstein's physics and principles of neuroscience tugged at me. Was this an epiphany? What if Gabrielle had stumbled onto a linking point between the human and the divine conversation, there in Blair, Nebraska, on an afternoon filled with feelings both of life and of death?

"You know," I said, grinning at the children, "there's actually something pretty profound in what you're saying, if we follow it all the way through. Though that follow-through might take some time, and a lot more research. But there's something very complex in the simplicity of what you've said."

They looked at me quizzically, which they often do when my words meander. Then we stood silently for a moment, taking in the view from the edge of the nursing home grounds in Blair, the sun beaming down on the green fields of Nebraska.

I thought, Okay, it's a given that we still can't really know what the soul becomes after death, but hadn't things changed since the times religious sacred texts were written, even in the past hundred years? *Wasn't there a way to know what the soul is composed of and how it works while the body is alive?* Because both science and religion have changed in the last decades, could it be that we are at a moment of truth as a civilization that we hadn't yet quite seized?

What was I thinking? I backtracked. Wait a minute. Was I, in an instant, conceiving of a way to provide a philosophical, religious, and scientific proof of the soul? Had I arrived at this idea by having a conversation with my children? If I had, how might this proof apply to children? It had grown, after all, from the wisdom of children.

It was very hot and very humid. Davita had had enough and asked to go back inside so we could return to their mother, Gail; Grandma Peggy; and the other family members still chatting with one another and Great-grandma Laura.

I led the girls back into the nursing home and up to room 214.

"Where did you go?" Grandma Peggy asked. She sat on the edge of her mother's bed, holding the aging matriarch's tiny hand.

"Just walking and talking outside," Gabrielle reported.

"We talked about *you*," Davita said, coming up to Great-grandma and giving her a kiss.

Instinctively wary that Davita might say something awkward like "we were talking about your dying," I said aloud, "We were actually being kind of philosophical—we were talking about the human soul and children."

Grandma Peggy ruffled Davita's hair. "You're a good soul, aren't you?"

Davita nodded, giving her grandma a hug.

Great-grandma Laura, looking first at my two daughters with her light blue, watery eyes, then looking to Gail and me, commanded, "You take good care of these two sweet souls, okay?"

"They are beautiful young lights, aren't they?" I said, my mind still on my thoughts of moments ago.

"Yes," she murmured. "They are. God lives in your children."

"We'll take good care of them," Gail assured her grandmother. I nodded my agreement, looking from my position at the foot of the bed into my two daughters' eyes, so beautifully lit from within—lit by the light of their own natures, by their sympathy for their elderly and dying progenitor, and by the light of God.

Everywhere around me hovered not only the souls of the dying but also those of young children. In my mind came a kind of verbal replay of the words "you're a good soul," "these two sweet souls," "God lives in your children." In these later moments of their long lives, Grandma and Great-grandma saw so clearly that near them stood not just "kids" but living, breathing *souls*—discernible aspects of God. Did this really mean anything? Or was all this just about words?

No, I didn't think so. There was something more here. In response to the comments from the girls' grandma and great-grandma, my epiphany increased to include a sense of the obvious light in my children's eyes—the same light in every child's eyes, and even beyond that light, the very essence of God.

The afternoon in Blair was a private epiphany, one I didn't share for quite some time even with my wife. But in it, this book began.

A VISION

We think of our children as "kids." What if we thought of them as *souls?* This was the challenge, inadvertently presented, by a ninety-five-year-old woman. Her words were not just a metaphor but, I think, a real description. As she moved toward death, Laura saw the soul of the child quite clearly.

Most of us are too busy to think of our children as being anything other than "boys" or "girls." This, like thinking of them as "kids," is worthy and important, but how little we think of them as *soul,* as *God,* as *infinite nature.* Laura seemed to see the infinite material. And even Gabrielle's and Davita's thoughts and words, which were touched by the circumstances around them that afternoon, seemed to have a consciousness of soul itself.

We think of our children as "offspring." How would it affect not only our methods of nurturing children but also the growth of our civilization if we spent much more of our time seeing our children as *infinite design?* How would this awareness change what a child means—not only to a parent, but also to human civilization? We think of our children as "young people"—what if we understood how richly and fully they were God?

These questions arose in me.

We are aware of how a child's body develops. What if we could also know how the actual divinity—the soul—of the child develops? If we had in our hands a blueprint of the invisible "spiritual" growth of divine identity, how would families and indeed our human cultures plot their courses for the lives of children and adults? Would it be different from the course we plot now? Would both wartime and peacetime be different? Would our hopes and dreams be, if not different, at least more achievable?

These questions occupied my mind over the next few days as I came to acknowledge—in the wake of our visit to Great-grandma Laura and my epiphany with my daughters outside the nursing home—the uniqueness of our place in human history. Both our scientific and religious knowledge have developed to a point of creating an astounding new vision, a vision that is right before our eyes but that has not yet been recognized. I came to realize that a number of incidents in my personal and professional life had built to this recognition and led to an unfolding of ideas and human stories that needed further scrutiny.

As the weeks and months progressed, this book, *The Soul of the Child,* emerged. Initially, it came as an epiphany only, for I needed to spend a great deal of time checking neurobiological as well as religious sources to make sure my vision did, indeed, make sense. I am grateful to all these sources for the book you are reading now, grateful especially that an in-depth study of both sets of sources reveals what my epiphany had hoped it would reveal: a distinctly new point in human possibility. And a new way of understanding our children.

THE BOOK

As a child development specialist, I have written this book so that any parent or caregiver of a child can find inspiration and practical wisdom in its insights. Simultaneously, as a student of both religion and science, I have written it in order to take our human understanding of the soul and God beyond where it has been before, to that place where science and religion can meet. Because the new neurosciences have reached a point of sophistication now, and because the world's religious literature is so readily available, via books, Internet, and teachers, we have come to a time in human history when the sciences of human nature and the metaphysics of divine nature can be seen running intertwined in the human project.

The Soul of the Child hopes to let you stand at the point of interconnection that human progress has created for us. At this point of connection, I hope you'll join me in noticing that a *new human* is emerging all around us. Our children are surely representative of that new human possibility.

As this book begins, we will discover the development of the human soul through a child's life. Gradually, we will come to see something startling, invigorating—that God is the child, and in being the child, God needs us far more than we've realized. The universe is, in fact, not merely a spiritual one-way street, wherein we need an omnipotent God and receive his aid, but a two-way street (at least) on which God, a beautiful child, needs us in beautiful and mysterious ways.

As the book progresses, I will present a new approach to the new sciences of neurochemistry, neurobiology, genetics, neurophysics, neuropsychology, and sociobiology ("the new sciences" will be our short name for these). I will also explore with you the millennia-old metaphysics of human religion (including references to nearly all world religions). In this unifying approach, I hope you'll discover how the human body, mind, and heart actually participate in the process religious metaphors have, for some time, named as *soul*. Once that discovery becomes second nature, everything changes, even our concept of God.

In Part I, I will offer a proof of the existence of soul, then reveal how the human soul develops and matures in children. From this point, I will offer a glimpse into the divine blueprint every child is born with. Even further in Part I, I hope to show you that the idea of a soul/body split, with which we've all grown up, is an erroneous idea promulgated by an earlier era—with the best of intentions, but one that is no longer necessary or even plausible. We are now able to observe—utilizing new PET (positron-emission tomography) technologies (as well as SPECT scans, MRIs, skin conductance tests, and more)—how completely, in the human lifetime, soul and body are one. The consequences of this new human ability are staggering; specifically, one outcome is that it brings us far closer to God—the divine activity of the universe—than we could imagine being before.

In this closeness you will find that many of the other dualities you and I have lived with throughout our childhood socialization and adult education will dissolve—mind versus brain, science versus religion, nature versus nurture. Given the new sciences available to us, it is possible now to see that we've been raising our children and living our lives with a script in mind, one written by a young civilization, in which history—both personal and cultural—is built upon a stage of oppositions. We will discover how different—how unified—the world looks when we penetrate beyond the veneer of these old, barely useful oppositions.

In Part II of this book, the new understanding we've gained of what soul is and how it operates in children will lead to a deeper understanding of the soul of the adult. Who are we really as adults? How do we lose soul and how can we regain it? There are clues all around us, clues we can understand better when we understand the soul of the child. There are spiritual messages religions have been sending us for thousands of years—concerning our lifelong divinity in human form—which now we can fully hear. As the book builds to its final chapter, we will come to realize one of the most inspiring revelations: Having understood the soul of both child and adult, we can now recognize the actual face of God. The two parts and six chapters within this book constitute a step-by-step proof of this ultimate idea: God is the Child.

The new sciences are changing our human script. I hope that this book will inspire you not only by showing how that script is changing, but also by showing how your life—especially as you care for children—can be one of leadership as humanity poises itself to navigate this sea change.

It is a sea change at the heart of the very definition of human nature.

THE NEW HUMAN

By the time you finish this book, you may recognize a new human among us. As we explore the soul of the child and the soul of the adult we will be compelled to notice, with great joy, evidence of our present human evolution from the genus and species we call *Homo sapiens*—an intelligent but xenophobic, brilliant but also warlike, human—to an even more sophisticated human being. In Part II of this book, we will name and fully explore this new human, providing the same genus name, *Homo*, but a new species name, *infiniens*, a new possibility.

We are in a sea change, if we will but recognize it—one that has been evolving for quite some time but most clearly during this last century. The technological and societal challenges of the last century have presented our lives with new challenges that our existing intelligence alone cannot face. We are evolving, as we always do, because of necessity. We are poised to learn of a new kind of intelligence by which to live life.

In exploring in this book the new human we are evolving into, our new intelligence, and our ability to know God, we will also discover the future of the family. What can we expect of the human family? What is the soul of the child asking of the human family? What can each of us do to protect the soul of the child? The answers to these questions lead to new expectations for children and for ourselves.

Arguably, the emergence of a new human—with a new way of looking at children, family, self, and life—is perhaps the single most important event in our current culture. It is also an event too little focused on by the human community. From the media, literature, and personal intuition we gain a fragmented sense that something new is going on, but we rarely integrate the fragments. *The Soul of the Child* offers an integration and focus grounded in our sense of the present and future of human childhood. As this book ends, we will circle back to where we will soon begin, at the point where human vision and intelligence, bound up in the mysterious and the holy, can provide our own hungry, truth-seeking souls with more than tradition and more than science fiction: a proof of the soul of the child that might, hopefully, impress an old woman who has seen it all.

Great-grandma Laura, who had lived a fruitful century, was experiencing the end of her life while her young progeny—myself and my daughters—were enlivened by a conversation and a vision of a new century. As Laura drifted off to sleep that afternoon, she closed her thin, almost transparent eyelids and inhaled and exhaled in that shallow way old people do. Outside the window lay the plains of

Nebraska with milo, corn, and wheat, windless and moist under an ember-colored sunset. In the halls of the nursing home were now mainly muted sounds—of human voices, of televisions, of footsteps. It became time for all of us to leave. We said good-bye to an old woman sleeping; we drove away, west, into an evening of yellow, red, and pink.

We did not know if Laura Whitcher, ninety-five, would live to see another afternoon gathering of her family. Driving from Blair to Lincoln, Nebraska, a trip that takes an hour and a half, we were subdued at moments, and happy at moments, the challenges and delights of family life weaving through our conversations and our silences.

Grandma, Grandpa, myself, Gail, and our two children had often made this car trip, and we enjoyed singing when we did so. Grandma Peggy requested that we sing the gospel song "Amazing Grace." And so that is what we did as we passed the town of Gretna, Nebraska, six souls singing together in a 1996 Oldsmobile 88. We sang for the living, and we sang for the dying.

I remember Laura Whitcher in every page of this book. I remember her and all the old people who have made possible the century of new discovery whose rewards we now reap. May this book do some justice to the nearly hundred years of life that not only one woman but also countless other men and women have given the world. Let us begin this book with the truth in mind that their lives speak loudly, if we will but listen, a message about the souls of the children they leave behind.

May Laura Whitcher continue her journey in peace, and may the message of her lifetime inspire us all.

PART I

The Soul of the Child

At the core of every human is an imperishable flame, the same energy that permeates all things— the fire of the comet, the twinkle of the stars.

—James A. Connor

1

THE SCIENCE OF THE SOUL: PROOF OF THE SOUL'S EXISTENCE

The human has no body distinct from the soul.

—WILLIAM BLAKE

Heavy snow fell that morning in 1990 outside Sacred Heart Hospital in Spokane, Washington. From our ninth-story room, my wife, Gail, and I could see the buildings of downtown Spokane, and the houses, pine trees, streets, and then hills north of the city.

We had been placed in a corner room of the maternity wing. Just outside our door were nurses going about their business; other families gathering; children running, walking, and squealing, and parents reining them in. "Come on, son! This way! Your mom's over in this room." Doctors' calls came over the ceiling speakers; a phone rang; a child of six or seven, a brown-haired girl wearing her winter coat, peeked into our room. Amid the din of children, adult voices, and hospital sounds, Gail and I could also hear silence, the hidden source of all sound. The wet flakes of snow outside the window seemed to bring the silence into our room and hold it there; for a few moments at a time, we would listen to the hush, holding hands, not talking, just waiting for a moment of truth, our first child's birth, on a February day. Despite our love for each other, our contemplation of silence would keep as Gail felt another painful contraction.

Gail was thirty-two, I two months from that mark. We had met at twenty-six, married at twenty-eight, moved to Ankara, Turkey, for two years, then returned to Spokane because, as Gail put it to me in our apartment in Ankara, "It's time to have children." We had been teaching in Turkey for just over a year and a half by the time she felt the call of the unborn child. The high window and the snow of the hospital in Spokane reminded me of the Ankara winter in which we often sat in our fourth-story apartment, overlooking other buildings and the snow-packed streets, anticipating parenthood.

"I want to carry a soul inside me," Gail had said. "I want to experience this back home, where I know the health care system better. I want to do it soon. I want to get started as soon as we get back to the States."

We talked over logistics, made plans, spoke our hopes aloud and thought them silently, and made our way back to the United States.

Gail got pregnant in the spring, a year and a half after the Ankara winter. Over the months, she wrestled with a complex pregnancy that included bed rest in the last weeks, but now here we were at Sacred Heart. Her water had broken the night before and contractions had begun. By phone, our doctor advised us to wait till morning to check into the hospital. We had waited, sleeping a little, then woke, prepared what we needed, got in the car, and arrived at 9:00 A.M. A nurse checked us in then guided us to our room. Gail changed into a hospital gown, then submitted to a number of fittings with hospital equipment: Different parts of her body were hooked up by an electrical cable to different monitors, some monitors revealing her and the baby's heart rate, some their temperature, others their blood pressure. Each monitor emitted, by means of green or white light, myriad revelations about the child ready to be born.

Gail was ending her time of carrying a soul inside her, and now that soul, connected to our outside world by scientific measurements of electrical impulse, spoke to her, the nurses, and all of us who gathered in support. It would be forty hours before our first child, Gabrielle, emerged from the womb, but emerge she did, healthy, and bringing Gail and me to tears.

THE MONITORS

For countless billions of years, organisms of many kinds—we humans being a recent addition to the long list—have remade themselves, conceiving offspring in whatever way nature made possible. We humans have painstakingly raised our offspring so that they could continue our immortality by becoming adults who, in turn, remade themselves.

Until very recently, we did not connect a mother and a fetus to electrical monitors. Birth occurred in the tundra, the savanna, the farmhouse, the family home, the car, or anywhere, for nature sometimes just won't wait.

When birth occurred elsewhere but a hospital, a pregnant mother's grandmas and aunties and midwives and doctors could read the signs of life inside the mother, and the mother herself could feel them internally, but we could not measure or see by ultrasound or read by electric waves the life hidden in the womb. We intuited an essential life in there, and religions and human socialization guided us to protect it at all costs, but we did not yet touch that life with a science capable of displaying, for medical use, the soul of the child within.

A few decades ago, that changed. Machines that read electrical signals were attached to pregnant mothers. Nearly everything about a child in utero can now be read. This change has given us the ability to read signals of life out of the hidden hush and silence from whence life comes. As I look back on those first moments of Gail's birthing process, when she was being hooked up to monitors, and as I think of myself, her, and others watching the green lines tweaking up and down, the silver lines cresting and troughing, the digital numbers reading out blood pressure, the sounds of beeps and drones, I see something I missed back then: Right before my eyes was a brilliant example of the new science of the soul that humanity is now learning.

Those monitors were reading not just my daughter's physical signals; *they were also reading her soul, the electrical energy that makes her physicality possible.* They read what we would later call "the light in her eyes"; they read her ability to move her limbs; they read fetal precursors to her quick intelligence, her moods, her hopes, and her dreams. All these things are *electricity,* and the monitors read that electricity quite well.

It was right in front of me when my own children were being born, but I missed it. It's right before all of us. To see it, we need not get more monitors hooked up. We need only do two things: look more closely, and give ourselves the permission to think differently than we did before it became possible to touch, with signs, the actual light that the soul is.

THINKING DIFFERENTLY ABOUT THE SCIENCE OF THE SOUL

By the end of this book—I hope, by the end of this chapter—you will say to yourself, I had thought I was a free thinker, but now I know better what freedom is. I hope you will say, I understand better what it means to find peace, within myself and in my world.

A great deal of our thinking, and thus our human energy, is caged in old ideas. Many of the problems we get into—within ourselves, in our communities, and on a larger scale, between nations and peoples—are the result of these ideas. I hope to introduce you to some new thinking and new ideas (some of which are, in fact, quite old but haven't been fully understood till now; and some of which are distinctly new).

Thinking differently takes us to a number of doorways, and behind each is a proof of the soul of the child that I hope will intrigue and touch you. Should you be a person who needs no proof of the existence of the soul, nor of its composition, you may be tempted to skip these next few pages. I hope you won't, for in them we will find beautiful and common ground.

Here are some new ideas this chapter will present:

- The soul and the body are not split but are one.

- Religion and science, which have historically been seen as oppositional to each other, actually teach us the same things about the soul.

- Though we think of ourselves as separate from God—God above and we below—in fact, we and God occupy the same space; knowing this cannot help but change our attitudes toward life, death, and nearly everything in between.

- At some level, each of us has already noticed evidence of the workings of the soul every day, even though we may lack the language and understanding to articulate what we've seen; once we do recognize our inherent, and relatively new, human ability to synthesize this information, we become a new human.

- We have been afraid to notice, with certainty, the physical composition of the soul, for we have thought that to equate soul and body might downgrade the mysterious workings of God; new discoveries help us see that God is not diminished but pleased by our progress in thinking and understanding.

- We may have been equally afraid to experience certainty because to fully know the soul of the child, and thus the intimacy of God, is to be required to reshape our human lives; this reshaping, the subject of the second half of this book, is a joyful but also a challenging task, one we've been putting off for many generations, for it will require changes in the way we live, and the way we act.

As this chapter proceeds, I hope you will come to see, as I have, that soul and body are not split; God is more than we thought; religion and science offer parallel proofs of the soul; the soul is a very physical phenomenon; and we, as a growing civilization, will make major leaps in human consciousness, and in the care of our children, when we fully understand who we are caring for, and thus, who we are.

Let us start this pattern of discovery with what religions have told us the soul is; then we will compare what religions have said to what science can now show us.

SEEING THE LIGHT

What have religions told us, since the beginning of oral and written language, about the soul, truth, and God? How have they spoken of soul, truth, and God in ways that we find echoed in neurobiological, scientific terms?

Both established religions and small, tribal spiritualities have always and in no uncertain terms called the soul, God, and truth "the light." What might they have meant? And could this light be what the monitors in the hospital during my children's births—and, indeed, during any medical procedure—have recognized, watched, and displayed?

Join me for a moment in noticing how clues to the human soul are locked in the human mind and thus are evident in humanity's historical teachings, songs, and ideas. The human mind creates itself everywhere in words, and words cannot create anything but the mind, for the mind (in the most expansive sense) is what the mind knows. It cannot know anything else. The mind makes what it knows. And it knows a secret: The soul is a measurable, yet still mysterious, light.

We find examples of this hidden in all religions.

Hinduism

Hinduism, the parent of so many other religions in Asia, makes no mistake about calling the soul "the light." A popular phrase when I lived in India—one that was brought over to the West in the later part of the last century—went like this: "May the light in me see the light in you." This phrase integrates the Hindu sense that we are "beings of light."

In the Hindu philosophy, our body cannot exist separate from our soul. The Hindu concept goes something like this: "Your body is an illusion, it is maya. Everything is actually soul. Without soul, you would be nothingness, darkness, unseen—the light is who you really are."

The Bhagavad Gita, the foundational text of Hinduism, refers to three modes of material nature. One of these, the mode of goodness, "being purer than the others, is illuminating." We will discuss later how "goodness" or moral action may well be a "whole brain activity" that "lights up the mind." The Gita, a teaching manual between the divine form, Krishna, and a young warrior, Arjuna, presents divinity as "seated in the hearts of all created, the light of the radiant sun."

Thus, in this ancient religion, not only is the individual person composed of light, but all of existence is also light itself.

Buddhism

In the *Mahaparinibbana Suttanta,* which recounts the end of the Buddha's life, we find the Buddha speaking: "Therefore, O Ananda, be ye lamps unto yourselves. Hold fast to yourselves as lamps."

In the Dharmapada, Buddha says, "The seeker who sets out

upon the Way shines bright over the world." The Way is the meditative development of a sense of one's own soul, which leads to the display of oneself as a radiant being, en-lightened within, and illuminating, by serving, the world.

Tibetan Buddhist Lama Surya Das explains: "Tibetan Buddhism teaches that at the heart of you, me, every single person, and all other creatures great and small, is an inner radiance that reflects our essential nature. . . . Tibetans refer to this inner light as pure radiance or innate luminosity; in fact, they call it ground luminosity because it is the 'bottom line.' This luminosity is birthless and deathless. It is a luminescent emptiness, called clear light, and it is endowed with the heart of unconditional compassion and love."

Judaism

Rebbe Nachman, an ancient Jewish thinker, taught that *devekuth,* God's counsel, should be the goal of our explorations in life—our Way. The experience of life itself, most notably of the joy and ecstasy of living, was to his mind the experience of "accepting God's counsel and thus, being caught up in God's light."

Nachman continues: "All of your future life is determined by what you find during the time of exploration. It all depends on how long your lamp can burn." The lamp again appears—this time in the West—as a descriptor for the soul.

In the Old Testament, God's conversation with Moses, which for all intents and purposes began the Jewish religion, takes place at a burning bush. Throughout Jewish lore, light and flame are God, in the same way that, at creation, God was Light. According to Jewish Cabalists, in order for Moses' soul to be able to hear God,

God had to make himself plain by becoming the original material of which Moses was composed: light.

In the Jewish sacred text the Zohar, the Book of Light, human souls are known to have come about this way: There was a huge explosion of Light, and once the explosion had finished, slivers of light were left everywhere. Those slivers were us, the living. You and I are each a sliver of light.

Christianity

Christianity is, of course, rife with references to the soul as light. In the Book of Matthew, Jesus preaches: "You are the Light for all the world. A town that stands on a hill cannot be hidden. When a lamp is lit, it is not put under a bushel basket but on the stand, where it gives light to everyone in the house."

Saul, who later became Saint Paul, discovered his "true self" while faced with an immense light, which temporarily blinded him. Jesus was in the process of crying out "Why do you persecute me?" when Paul "saw the light." In seeing God's light, Paul knew his own soul completely.

The Christian poet Dante, in the *Purgatorio*, presents the soul as a beloved female figure, Beatrice. Depicting a man's soul as a beautiful woman was a literary convention of the day. Even more interesting is how he associated this soul with light. As Dante writes in the voice of his instructive mentor, Virgil: "Save all questions of consequence till you meet her who will become your lamp between the truth and mere intelligence."

Saint Augustine wrote in his *Confessions* of both the soul and God as light, fire, flame, and the lamp. In one case, Augustine refers to God and the soul as one—the light. In this passage, he refers to his youthful ignorance of God's true word. "At that time of igno-rance, as you, the light of my heart, do know, your apostolic words were still not known to me." In another of his myriad, similar "light references," he cries for his soul: "The light is clouded over! But look! It is before us!"

Referring to his own ignorance of the truth, he confesses, "I did not know that [the soul] must be enlightened by another light in order to be a partaker in the truth . . . for you will light my lamp, O Lord my God, you will enlighten my darkness. . . . For you are the true light, which enlightens every one in this world."

In Catholic churches, and in nearly all other places of religious observance worldwide, the lighting of candles and lamps is another indication of the human intuition that luminosity—radi-ance and light—is germane to our divine composition. Perhaps in Christianity, candle flames and candles symbolize the soul because of Bible stories surrounding the Apostles' apprehension of the Holy Spirit—when the Holy Spirit appeared, tiny flames danced on each of their heads. No matter where the source of the symbol, in nearly every world religion, flame is soul, soul is flame.

Islam

In Zoroastrianism, a root religion of Islam (as well as other reli-gions), the "God" is Ahura Mazda, the Unquenchable Flame. Individual souls issue from the original light.

This "love of light" is very true in Islam as well, where the candle flame, in the religious poetry of Háfiz and Jalal al-Din Rumi, is directly linked to soul. Muslim texts, most especially the Koran, are filled with constant references to light. Sura XVIII, The Cave, provides one of the richest, multilayered uses of light.

In this Sura, young men must seek refuge from persecutors in a dark cave, wherein they become closer to God. God's guidance is felt as light; furthermore, illumination of the self is light; knowledge of one's own soul and love of and by God is light; and God's power is light. In this Sura, we find the idea that is implied in every religion: Not only is the soul light, but also God is light. This is a hint of what will be developed much further in this book—that if we are light, and God is light, and our children are light, we have stumbled upon a great idea, which creates a new way of viewing the human.

The Islamic daily prayer cycle itself is based in the sun's light cycle. Muslims pray five times a day—*Fajr*, the dawn prayer; *Zuhr*, the noon prayer, or just after the sun has reached its greatest height; *Asr*, the afternoon prayer, when the sun is halfway down; *Maghrib*, prayer at sunset; and *Isha*, night prayer, which transpires after the sun has set and when darkness is all around. Not surprisingly, given the light-orientation of Islam, *Isha* symbolizes death. The soul's light has left the body, metaphorically speaking, in *Isha*. Night prayers focus on the return of the soul's light.

Awwal, the state of being in which Creator is fully creation, a personal sense of adoration is reached as one realizes: "O Allah, you are the infinite open ray of light!"

Jalal al-Din Rumi, perhaps the most popular Muslim poet of all time, uses metaphors of light, including fire, countless times to refer to the soul and God.

In one case, using "I" as the Beloved God and "you" as a searcher, he writes:

You are burning up your soul to keep the body delighted, but you don't know what you're doing. I am another kind of firelight.

Khalil Gibran, the Lebanese-born poet whose book *The Prophet* has touched millions of hearts, writes:

I have found that which is greater than wisdom.
It is a flame spirit in you ever gathering more of itself.

Goddess Religions

Most religious traditions are based on texts written by males and are structured such that males are the primary celebrants. But there is also a long tradition of female, Goddess religions, which we've all learned a great deal about in the last few decades. Do the Goddess religions create a different picture of the soul than do the traditional patriarchal religions? Though there are many differences between these types of religions, they both agree that a human being is light. In Goddess traditions, the light of the moon is often more active than the light of the sun, but that light is still the source of being.

In the beginning there was darkness, then the light, say nearly all the creation stories of all the religions. An African Goddess creation tale has this opening: "There was darkness, like the inside of a rock, and then it was as if the rock of the world shattered, and all was light. All the souls of the Great Mother poured forth from the light."

Shamanism

Shamanism is the general term used for native theologies, aboriginal worldviews, and tribal religions. Shamans are the equivalents of priests, rabbis, priestesses, and healers.

Medicine men and women are famous examples of shamans.

Tribal cultures gain their religious and spiritual understanding not only from life experience but also from shamans; thus the cultures are called shaman-based, or shamanic, in the same way the West is known as being Judeo-Christian.

Shamanic religions resemble Goddess religions in that they tend to be more "earth-based" than are the "sky-based" monotheistic religions. God, Allah, and Jesus are people of the sky, we might say, in comparison to Mother Earth, Grandfather Rock, or She Who Talks with Wind. While Father Sky is an important part of shamanic religions, he does not dominate them in the way the Father God dominates Western religion.

Shamanic religions are filled with original human mythology, living examples of the ideas that monotheistic religions borrowed millennia ago.

Not surprisingly, in shamanic culture, light and soul are one and the same.

Shamanic folk tales, for instance, are filled with references to darkness becoming light. In one Native American tale, the world is created by Coyote falling into a dark pit, discovering a flaming branch, then bringing this flame out of the pit: from this, life was created. Every living soul, according to this Plains story, is a flame of light.

Among the natives of the Andes Mountains, most notably the Incas, we find the practice of *paq'o* initiation. A person goes through a number of trials—life trials and ritualized ordeals— along a journey toward spiritual maturity. A spiritually mature person, a *paq'o,* is defined as one able to visualize the fields of energy that constitute each being. These fields, invisible to an uninitiated or spiritually immature individual, are quite lit up for the *paq'o*. The spiritually mature person, or shaman, learns how to "read the light," then how to interact with every person as a "field of light."

Philosophies of the Soul

Religions have dealt directly with what soul is, and religions have influenced the minds of philosophers who did the same. The discipline of philosophy, as a companion to religion, has been defining the human soul for millennia.

Aristotle, for instance, argued that the soul could be found "throughout the body." For him, the soul was a light under every part of our skin—it was the light of all cells and organs.

Aristotle may well have been responding to something he didn't like in Plato's ideas about the soul. For Plato, the soul was an Ideal, a kind of living idea, that existed in a state of transmutability—it could change all the time—until it entered the darkness of the body, becoming "the pilot of the body, as a charioteer is the pilot of the horses who pull his chariot."

Saint Augustine, who was both a religious figure and a social philosopher, and Saint Thomas Aquinas, one of the most famous philosophers in our history, each lived as philosophical bookends to the Middle Ages—Augustine at the beginning of that time, Aquinas toward the end. Augustine melded Christianity and Platonic ideas, seeing the body as being piloted by the soul, which God places, or "breathes" into us. Aquinas imagined the soul more complexly and was one of the first philosopher-scientists to try to imagine how this cosmic breathing actually might feel in our cells. He proposed that the soul was like light breathing throughout ourselves, like having God within us.

René Descartes, the seventeenth-century philosopher famous for concluding "I think, therefore I am," argued that the soul was actually located near or in the pineal gland, and was lit up enough for a few people, people of extraordinary gifts, to see there.

These are just a few of the concepts of the soul that can be found in our Western philosophical tradition. But they all have one thing in common: The soul is depicted by the philosopher-scientist as a "spark."

"The soul is the spark of existence."

"The soul is the spark of light within us."

"God planted a spark within us, then breathed wind onto it, giving us life."

In these last few pages, I have tried to display something that has perhaps been right before our eyes for generations, but which we were not fully aware of: All religions and philosophies, while seemingly "culturally separate" creations that use different metaphors to express ideas about the human soul, have in fact been revealing the same truth—whether in the mountains of India or Tibet, the burning city of Carthage, the Greek empire, or in the Hebrew, Christian, Moslem, or Goddess traditions. We might even say that the idea that God is light, that the soul is light, that we are light, is burned into the human psyche.

Now what shall we do with this displayed idea? It is a piece of a puzzle. How shall we utilize it?

THE SCIENCE OF THE SOUL

Let us utilize it this way: Whether in world religions or in the history of philosophy, the soul is known as light, or as a spark, and now the new sciences can show us why.

What Is Light?

First, what do we know today about this light our ancestors called the soul? What do we know about *light itself?* We keep using the word *light*—but what do we know about this light, which as soul is obvious to us, yet still so mysterious?

As neurophysics researcher Joel Achenbach puts it: "There has been light from the beginning. There will be light at the end. In all its forms—visible and invisible—it saturates the universe. . . . Light reveals the world to us. Body and soul crave it. Light sets our biological clocks. Light feeds us, supplying the energy for plants to grow. . . . Light is more than a little bit inscrutable. Modern physics has sliced the stuff of nature into ever smaller and more exotic constituents, but light won't reduce. . . . Our lives are built around light, our daily existence is continuously shaped—and made vivid—by that ambiguous stuff that dates from the beginning of time."

We know this fascinating fact about light: It has no volume. This means it needs other shapes and things of mass by which to show itself. Even when a beam of light shines, its hidden qualities are not revealed unless it is placed against a mass. For instance, every beam of light carries every color in the spectrum, but we don't see these colors unless the light is shot into a prism; only through the reflection in the mass of the prism do we see an aspect of the nature of the light.

We know this too: Light is both a particle and a wave.

We know that the speed of light is constant for all observers.

We also know that at the speed of light there is no time. Albert Einstein was the first to fully understand and prove this. At the speed of light, time stops.

We know that light can be guided. Charles Townes and Arthur Schawlow developed the LASER (light amplification by stimulated emission of radiation) in order to utilize the possibility of cohering light into a narrow beam. The uses of this narrow beam, from medical surgeries to telescopes, are infinite.

We also know that all human communication technologies are based on manipulating not just sound but also light. Technology expert George Gilder put it this way: "Light was made by God for communications."

This, then, is a little about light. How shall we connect what science knows about light with what human wisdom has taught us?

The New Science of Neurochemistry

The science of neurochemistry shows us that the human being, like all living things, *is only alive in relation to the electrical energy— the light—it organizes.* We are electromagnetic energy, vibrating, luminous, flowing, and quicksilver. The very neurochemistry of human life is electrical—a spark, a flow of light. It is a volumeless, fast-moving, minute spectacle of light.

In the same way that a lightbulb illuminates when we throw the wall switch, or a candle flame burns when lit, living beings are alive with light. PET scans now show us that every action and every thought is composed of electrical energy. We process electrical signals while walking in a park, experiencing sensations from wind, light, trees, or from television signals, walls, airplanes, the taste of curry or hamburgers, the thousand smells around us, noticed or unnoticed. All are electrical energy stimulating human sense organs, then through them, the brain, then the brain stimulating the human nervous, respiratory, and circulatory systems. The circle of electrical energy a human being participates in is an endless circle of electrical stimulation. We experience the stimulants and the electricity, though we don't call them electricity—we call them "feelings," "smells," "actions," or "words"—but they're all electricity. They're all light. Whether a galvanic skin response test is administered to our bodies, or an EKG to our heart rate, or a PET scan to our brain waves, or a series of monitors to a mother's full uterus, all will measure that light.

When the electrical energy is gone, we all know instinctually that death has occurred. More than anything we fear losing that circle of electric energy, because to lose the spark of light—the electrical energy—is to be deleted (at least so we fear) from all of existence and nature as we know it.

For this reason great thinkers have argued in favor of a split between the soul and the body, a split that has, as we will see in a moment, kept us from fully caring for our children and for ourselves. Suffice it to say that just because death appears to exist does not necessarily mean the soul and the body are split. Soon I will show what I mean.

First, however, let us look a little more closely at the workings of the electromagnetic energy that is the ground of our being—the spark, the light, the lamp that is soul and body as one.

The Body

Your child's small body operates by virtue of cell activity; it *is* cell activity. A slug inching across your sidewalk also experiences cell growth and cell activity, but in a more simplistic way than you or your child do. A slug's life is termed, in neurochemistry, "simple cell activity," and human life is termed "complex cell activity." Your child is a complex of cell activity that is built on the same basic type of cell activity of all natural life.

The atoms that constitute each individual cell, as you may remember from high school physics, are composed of protons, neurons, electrons, and even quarks and newly discovered quantum particles. Not surprisingly, protons, neurons, electrons, and quarks are all electromagnetic energy in a constant process of vibration. When Aristotle found the soul "throughout the body," he knew neither about complex cell activity nor about quarks, but he sensed that the whole body was lit up with vibratory resonance; and he was right. The human body is a mass of electrical impulses.

The Brain

These impulses need an organizer, which is the brain. A mass of lit-up cells, the brain is small in an infant but grows to approximately three-and-one-half-pounds in an adult. The brain is composed of neural networks of axons and dendrites connected by synapses, which interact among themselves through neurotransmitters. Not surprisingly—these neurotransmitters travel—*at or near the speed of light.*

The brain is divided into three major areas:

- The brain stem, which is the basic survival brain, emits signals for human digestion, breathing, and the fight-or-flight instinct (when I'm scared I'll either confront my aggressor or run).

- The limbic system, which takes in sensory information and sends signals, including our hormonal signals, to the rest of the brain, generates most of our emotional processing.

- The four lobes at the top of the brain (the parietal at the top of the head, the occipital at the back, the temporal on both sides, and the frontal just behind the forehead), which we call, for short, the neocortex, make us capable of advanced, uniquely human reasoning such as making moral decisions, speaking a language, having abstract thoughts, reading, composing music, and so on.

The three parts of the brain run on electromagnetic current, and every connection that is made among them is made by filaments of light—neurotransmitters and synapses among axons and dendrites. There are countless signals flowing through the brain at one time, most being memories or echoes of previous experiences we've had. In order for a single thought to occur, hundreds of thousands of neurons must vibrate as electrical pulses move throughout the brain.

Is this the candle flame? Is this the flame spirit, the infinite open ray of light?

The Brain-Body Systems

The connection between this small electrical mass in the head we call the brain and the larger electrical mass we call the body is made via the sensory, nervous, circulatory, and respiratory systems. Signals come in through these systems and activate the brain, which then responds to them.

A little boy or girl hurts a knee playing soccer. The soccer game, the desire to play soccer, the collision with the other player, the nerve-ending pain reaction, the emotions and feelings, the call to a parent for help—all are electrical signals that run from the environment to the senses, body systems, and the brain, and then back again. They all can be traced as electrochemical light particles.

Is this not what was meant by "your soul is a lamp" or "the soul is slivers of light"?

The neuroscientist Andrew Newberg, coauthor of *Why God Won't Go Away*, gives the following example of this process vis-à-vis sensory information. "The basic functional unit of the human nervous system is the neuron, the tiny, spindly cell that, when arranged into intricately woven chains of long neural pathways, carries sensory impulses to the brain. At the basic level, sensory data enters the neural system in the form of billions of tiny bursts of electrochemical energy gathered by countless sensors in the skin, eyes, ears, mouth, and nose. These neural impulses race along neural pathways, cascading like a line of falling dominoes, leaping synaptic gaps and triggering the release of chemical neurotransmitters as they carry their sensory messages."

Because electrochemical neurons and other such particles exist everywhere in the human system, were we to place a child's whole body on a body scan, no experience or reaction in the child would occur that could not be detected via electric impulse: via light.

The Exterior of the Body

Usually when we use the term "body," we mean all that is contained within the skin. But the science of neurochemistry extends this definition to also include the heat put out by the body; thus we can detect the soul not only *in* the body but also around it, along its edges. From ancient shamans to modern health care professionals, many have long been aware of the soul around the outside of the body. Technology can now show us the electrical current that has been called our "aura." When scanned by infrared technology, bodies are shown to give off light and heat.

Most of us have not actually used infrared technology ourselves, but we've probably seen an action film in which a character such as a soldier can't fulfill his mission unless he is able to see human targets at night. After the soldier places infrared goggles over his eyes, his targets—which had been indiscernible to the naked eye in the darkness of night—now show up because of their body heat.

People often think that infrared technology is picking up only the heat emanating from within the body, that is, the heat "inside it" or "beneath the skin." But infrared technology picks up the haloed *outline,* or "haloed exterior," of the body as well. The heat emanating from the body is, in fact, not only contained under the skin but is also released beyond the skin, around the exterior body.

Native American touch healers, who during prayer states move their hands about an inch above a prone body without any visible physical contact, are touching not the skin and bones of the body but the halo, the electric currents of body heat, invisible to the naked eye—heat expressed and emanated by the contained, fast-moving electricity within the physical body we call a human being.

Is this not the soul around the body, which is depicted in religious paintings as a glowing halo around a human being?

THE SOUL RIGHT BEFORE OUR EYES

Having looked at some of the ideas from both religion and science, is it not possible now to say that no matter which technology is used, your child will show evidence of the soul? Do not the brain, the physique, body systems, and body heat all appear as light? Having raised this truth to consciousness, does it not become easier to remember that within that child (and within yourself) *there is actually no separation among brain, nervous system, body, and body heat?* The disconnect between "soul" and "body" lies only in our perception, our thinking. In reality, we are all electrical currents processing life at the speed of light, without separation among brain, nervous system, limbs, and halo.

The soul, we might say, is right before our eyes. Perhaps it has always been so, but because we did not have the technology to fully understand the interconnection of soul and body—the complete unity of them in light—we perceived a split between soul and the body. We need no longer struggle with that split. Now we can scan the human, using PET, SPECT, and other technologies, similar to those that monitored Gail and our baby. Now we can see that the human being is light itself.

I would go even further to argue that we can see the essential, luminous unity of soul and body even if we don't have access to PET scans or infrared technologies. Various scientific technologies have provided physical and empirical evidence of the existence of the soul, which religions and philosophy have always posited. But you don't need to be a doctor or brain tomography technician, nor have your baby in a hospital, to "see the light" that is the base composition of your child.

The spark, the light, the slivers of light, the vibrating pulses of light, the heat—that soul of the child—are inherent in our experience of the child, as the soul of a human is inherent in our experience of any human.

Let's recall some types of experiences we've all had that might make this most clear.

Perhaps you have felt the soul of another when you feel sexual "heat" emanating from your lover. You can physically feel that body heat, that love or even lust, and it is very real because hormones and pheromones are coursing not only through your lover's body but also emanating from it at the speed of light.

Perhaps you've felt the heat too when you reach for your child and sense the amazing heat a little body puts out. You are feeling not only the heat within the body but also the electrical heat expressed by the body's systems.

Not only when you feel the heat of your child's body but also when you look into your child's eyes, the electricity of soul is quite clear, especially in the lit, candlelike quality of the eyes. World traditions guide us to call the eyes "the windows to the soul" because we see the soul, at an instinctive level, in our children's eyes, and in the eyes of most people around us.

We also see "soullessness" when we look into the eyes of people who are evil (we will explore the neuroscience of evil more completely in Chapter 3). Perhaps the first thing a person notices about a Ted Bundy or another mass murderer is "cold eyes." If you read crime novels, something I do to relax during summer vacations, you will notice that most serial killers are described as having cold eyes. When an actor depicts an evil person, he generally forces a coldness into his eyes. For instance, John Malkovich, in the espionage thriller *In the Line of Fire,* with Clint Eastwood, rarely blinks, and looks out at the world without emotional warmth. In *The Silence of the Lambs,* psychopath Hannibal Lecter, played by Anthony Hopkins, has the coldest eyes that great actor can manage.

These "cold eyes" are very real, neurochemically: They lack, in simple terms, the normal heat that light—moving rapidly and generating complex, active waves—gives off. The brains of psychopaths are minutely lateralized in comparison to those of normal people, that is, they compartmentalize activity into fewer parts of the brain. When we explore this more fully later, you will get a clearer sense than you may have had of why you get goose bumps and feel visceral fear at the sight of a psychopath's cold eyes.

The warmth or coldness in a person's eyes is an easy way of experiencing, in everyday life, the light the soul is. But what if you are blind? Can you still "see" the soul?

Yes. Blind people utilize touch to experience the soul of another, feeling through the skin of their fingers not only the contours of a face but also the body heat put off by another. In utilizing touch, blind people don't look into someone's eyes to discover a window to the soul but, instead, feel another's heat and body to gain a sense of the soul they have met. Blind people can have uncanny intuitions about the moral character of others and yet never see into others' eyes, intuitive proof that the soul is multifaceted and "visible" to the touch.

It is possible, also, to notice that any of us can experience the certainty of soul by using our ability to touch.

When your infant daughter reaches to clamp her fingers around your finger, she is using a physical gesture to ask you to recognize her as the spark of life you adore. Your adoration of her *physically increases her electrical energy,* and in turn, *the quantity and quality of her electricity of emotion in the limbic system;* this increase instructs her digits to clamp harder, so that you will increase your electromagnetic adoration, your light, even more.

When your child runs toward you and gives you a hug, you feel an electric jolt of pleasure. This joy is your electrochemical reaction to your child's love. It is a blending of two electrical fields. The biochemist Rupert Sheldrake, one of the first to identify living beings as energy fields, calls human beings "fields of light." In his terms, I and my child are, in the hug, two fields of light immersed in each other.

We all feel this electricity of love as little electric shocks all the time—and we especially yearn to feel those electric shocks when we are away from our loved ones. We say to the person next to us on the airplane or the train, "I can't wait to get home to see the light of my children's eyes." We long for the joyful feeling of connection between ourselves and our children. This feeling is experienced on the cellular level as one of electromagnetic, luminous connectivity. It is remembered by the brain as a tactile connection—a hug, a kiss, or a caress—and stored as much more. It fills the memory, activating the limbic system expansively, driving us to get home to our loved ones. All this happens as electrical current, both in our own minds and memories, and between ourselves and our children or partner upon reunion.

When we are sad, we seek "the light at the end of the tunnel." Think about when you are lonely—you feel "low," "blue," "encased in darkness." In an immensely imaginative novel by James Stoddard, called *The High House*, the narrator writes: "The constant dreariness had sunk into his soul and he would have given much for a real ray of sunshine." In another passage: "The grey clouds left all subdued, drained of light and life." This is the experience we all have—thus it is constantly written this way in books. Dreariness, depression, and darkness yearn for light.

If visual and tactile ways of noticing the soul are the two ways we think of most quickly, sound comes next to mind. We constantly sense the electromagnetic pulsing in sounds, though we may not realize it. Sound is a form of light. What do we mean?

When you coo at your infant son, he picks up the electrical signal of sound in the parietal lobe, which then causes another cavalcade of electric pulses, causing him to coo back. The aural stimulation simply can't happen without life being "lit" in each of you—electrochemical vibration. Sound is electrical vibration. In Hinduism and ancient Judaism the religious equivalent of the big bang—creation—is sound and light together, the explosion of creation being depicted as the emergence of light from darkness and the divine voice from nothingness. Among the Christian disciples during Pentecost, the Sound of God is a rushing wind (the Holy Spirit).

The Greek philosopher Pythagoras was perhaps the first scientific thinker to promulgate the idea that sound and light are partners, an idea that is verified in the modern physics of sound. In Pythagoras's view, everything was composed of sound—electrical vibrations. "And all these sounds and vibrations form a universal harmony, in which each element, while having its own function and character, contributes to the whole." Ancient Hindu doctors, in turn, believed that the human body had seventy-two thousand *nadis*—energy channels analogous to nerves—by which sound traveled, and which could be used in healing. Science has verified the existence of even more than seventy-two thousand nerve channels by which sound can be carried.

In ancient Judaism, Christianity, and Islam, the "sound" God made when he created life was the sound of "breath." God breathed life into the world, bringing light with that breath. This is the sound of electrochemistry. The act of breathing is directly linked to the expression of light in the human body. As air is inhaled and exhaled, it floods our cells with electrochemical activity. Aboriginal shamans in Australia believe that people must put their hands to their mouths when they're astonished so they don't lose their souls. These shamans fear that as "the breath leaves the body, so will the light."

We've looked at ways that the light we are calling soul, this soul we are calling light, is experienced by us both through technological devices and in everyday life—monitors, PET scans, infrared technologies, touching a child's finger. There is still another way we instinctively know the light. We know when the electric current of life, the heat in a person's senses and feelings, is gone. Gradually the light seems to leave an aging person's body—Great-grandma Laura, or any other who, right before our eyes, seems to be gradually diminishing. There are other times, as well, when death comes suddenly; we do not have the time to watch the soul gradually diminish. These are times of quick death. At a memorial service for those who died in the September 11, 2001, terrorist attacks on the World Trade Center, a minister spoke these words as he spread sacramental incense: "Eternal rest grant unto them, and may perpetual light shine upon them." The emotion we all felt, whether at the site or in the television audience, was like an electric current, made even more powerful by the truth in his words—our felt sense that the dead were, though no longer living in our realm of perception, nonetheless light itself.

BEYOND THE SOUL/BODY SPLIT

Whether you look into a child's eyes, feel her tiny fist, or hear his coo, you know, instinctually and by human instruction, how to refract back the light of love your child is showing you. I am saying in this chapter that when all metaphors, and even feelings of love, move aside, we are left simply with the electricity itself.

And that is not a reduction but an invitation to greater wisdom. In this wisdom, we discover that neurochemistry is showing us a way beyond the soul/body split. *There is no human cell not composed of the current, the light, the candle flame.* The electrical impulses that vibrate in and through us are soul. Our bodies are our souls too. It is not even necessary to use the terms "body" and "soul" except as metaphors.

This is a neurochemical circling back to the original conceptions of human life.

When Hinduism and Buddhism insist that the body is an illusion, they are using a metaphor to express what is a fact: Soul and body are one.

When the Jews, the Christians, and the Muslims all insist that we are the light of the world, they are insisting in metaphor what is a fact: We are light, whether one uses the word *soul* or the word *body* to define us.

When Native tribes, aborigines, and members of Goddess religions and shamanic cultures insist that there is no separation among a human, a deer, a leaf, a rock—for all these "things" are made of one material, the Great Mother—they are insisting in metaphor what is a fact: Separations are illusions, especially separations between what is divine and what is material.

Still, many of us will continue to have the notion that there is, in fact, a split between soul and body. It just feels right to think it. Not only has this idea been a part of Western thought for millennia, but doesn't the existence of death create the need for a soul/body split? The body dies—mustn't the soul remain alive? Since the soul remains alive when the body dies, mustn't the soul and the body be made of different materials, and thus not be the same divine material—or, at least, mustn't one be more divine than the other? At death the electricity, the light that we are, leaves the body. But it cannot be destroyed, given that it is energy, which can only be transformed not eradicated. So we are back to the soul/body split.

Or are we?

Inherent in the idea of a soul that is not quite a body and a body that is not quite a soul is also another idea: We can only think of soul and body one way. What if we could mature our minds to the point of realizing there is another way? What if we could stretch our minds such that they could accept two seemingly opposing ideas at once and also realize that they are not contradictions?

Accomplishing this would be an example of polylogical thinking. Our culture's reasoning process, however, is currently based mainly on monological thinking. We tend to search for one idea that explains everything, whether it's why our child turned out a certain way ("Because he wasn't fed breast milk") or why a business deal went badly ("Because I wasn't better prepared for the meeting"), when in fact there are many other reasons for each result. Because it is hard to track many reasons, we track one.

As this book develops, we will move deeply into polylogical thinking—the thinking of the new human, thinking that goes beyond our previous definitions of intelligence, into a new kind of spiritual intelligence. For now, let us simply keep in mind the possibility that all three of these things might be true:

- The soul and the body, during this lifetime of breath, are one.

- The soul, as light, is also capable of existence without a human body.

- These two ideas are in no way contradictory.

As we move into the next chapter, we will in fact discover that to eschew this kind of polylogical thinking is to bring peril upon ourselves, especially upon our children.

Speaking of the deeds we do and the spiritual context in which we do them, the popular Lebanese poet Kahlil Gibran writes how illogical it is for us to think that the actions of our bodies are separate from those of our souls: "Who can spread his hours before him, saying, 'I do this for God and this for myself; this for my soul, and this other for my body'?" We do everything for God, Gibran teaches. Everything we are is soul.

To exist without this idea, we will find, is to exist in eternal conflict between the material world and the spiritual world; it is to lose ourselves, our children, and those we love in a war between flesh and spirit. It is, ultimately, to disrespect the divinity of God's creation: matter, flesh, self, and child. Inherent in our monological thinking about soul and body is, we will notice, a hidden and inappropriate disgust for matter and for flesh, and a resultant idealization of an invisible soul, which leads to a painful result: Thinking the light of God to be not of this world, we do not nurture the light of God fully in this world.

WHERE WE GO FROM HERE

If your faith in the existence of the soul has never faltered; if your understanding of the sacredness of every human life and every moment of that life has never been stronger; and if your belief that the body is God's temple has always been complete, you may think to yourself, Why has it been necessary to prove the existence of the soul? Why has the author taken the time to begin a multilayered, book-long argument with the idea that the soul and body are one? You might think, I already know my children and I and all beings are children of God, so why has the author written of a deep coherence between religion and science regarding the soul of the child?

When I watched my wife get strapped up to the neuro-electrical monitors in our child's birth room, I was a young, excited man seeking to be fully present to the occasion, my emotions bounding between fear ("Will Gail and the baby be all right?") and joy ("There's never been a moment like this!"). I followed orders, helped Gail breathe, got out of the way during the "transition" phase, when she became angry, stayed as close as possible through all phases, and when it was time, cut Gabrielle's umbilical cord.

I saw a little girl's body come out of Gail's adult body. I did not, except perhaps in the most unconscious sense, see a soul. At some deep unconscious level I certainly must have experienced my child as light itself, for my joy, like a luminescence inside me, welled up into tears as I held her. I know Gail's did too, as did the joy of others present, from a nurse who had befriended us, to our children's godmother and godfather.

Yet I did not realize the light *consciously,* and even more troubling to me, I did not—until the conversation at Great-grandma's nursing home—realize the divinity, the actual soul of my two children, in every moment of their lives. I had, for most of the days and nights of their lives, lots else to do. I knew my children as mainly bodies to be transported to the bus, to school, to friends' houses, to sports activities; I had known my children as economic interns that I must train to "make it in the world." When I thought of them as souls, it was in regard to getting them to Sunday school, or providing them with "time in nature," or time in character development experiences. I had not integrated a sense of soul into my own children's lives, *even despite the fact that I am a man of religion.*

Am I unusual? Don't most of us fall into this trap? Don't we miss the soul of our spouse, our coworkers, our friends, our children? We tend to. We are focused on other things.

Perhaps for that reason more than any other, I have provided the picture of soul you've read in this chapter. We need the picture—we need to connect the dots. We need to see the truth that is right before us: Our children are not just "kids"—they are light itself.

We think of our children as "kids who are doing sports." As this book proceeds, I hope you'll come to think of their sports activity as *divine play*.

We think of our children as "going to school to get good grades." I hope you'll soon think of your children's learning as their active engagement in knowing their own and the world's divinity.

In a culture as busy and competitive as ours, we think of children as success objects, pushing them to "succeed at all costs." I hope you'll join me in thinking more than perhaps you have about their divine *destiny* as souls, and their inherent right to live a life of *meaning, spiritual purpose, and mission*.

We think of our children as "ours." What if we thought of them as long-standing souls, whom we have only *borrowed* for a few years, as light is borrowed, not owned?

We think of our children as bodies because so much of what we must do for them involves, from the first day of life, care of their bodies. I hope you'll soon think of your children, yourself, and all around you as light itself, which needs to be cared for not only as body but also as soul.

Won't these kinds of rethinking lead us to realize how much more we can do to make children's lives holy, and our own lives more meaningful?

I hope by the end of this book you will not only answer this question in the affirmative but also know how to activate your answer. Bonding and attachment to children is only complete when we know and attach to the *soul* of the child too. This is a crucial element in human development that you and I are best suited to give the soul of the child; more than that, it is an element on which all of human life depends, and an element not well enough understood today.

This secret element, this treasure, whose actual growth we can observe in the next chapter through the science of neurobiology, is if not the source of the light itself, then at least the very air, the oxygen, that keeps the human candle lit.

2

THE SOUL GROWS: SOUL DEVELOPMENT FROM BIRTH TO ADULTHOOD

When I was born, I saw the light, yet still the life I
live is the perpetual surprise that I exist.

—RABINDRANATH TAGORE

A baby lies in a crib, looking up at a mobile that dapples the
room in dazzling, flashing sunlight from the window nearby.
The baby's mother walks into the room, watching the quick
patches of light on the white walls, the crib rail, the child's smiling
face. The child transfers its attention from the sunlight and mobile
to the mother, whose smile and long arms are so inviting. The
mother takes the child out into the living room, where now there is
the dazzle of people talking. The mother shows the child to her
gathered friends, each of whom holds the baby, cuddles, coos,
admires. Then, after a while, the baby feels overwhelmed by all the
attention, pushing little fists to eyes, turning the head to the left,
threatening to cry. So many smells, sounds, flashes—it's time for
mom again. The mother takes the child back, holds tight, accepting
the crying as a part of the moment. She returns the child to the crib,

wraps the baby in very tight swaddling, so that the child feels safe again. The baby lies back, tears receding, as the mobile's flashes of light reappear, like slivers of tumbling, whirling air.

This baby has experienced, within a set of minutes, the absolute calm of the crib and the sweet observances made possible by solitude, then the longing for others, the adoration of others, and then the discomfort of being with others. As if the baby were hooked up to the mother by electrical monitors, the wise and intuitive mother reads the baby's signals very well. The mother knows how to care for this light of her life. She knows when the child's senses are overstimulated. She gives her child quiescence and activity, aloneness and relationship. She is a mother who knows beautiful and profound *attachment* with her child. For her, there is no light or life in the universe without her child. If she lost this child, she would prefer darkness and death to life.

Somewhere else in the same city, a baby lies in a crib, beneath a mobile that dapples the room with dazzling, flowing patches of refracted sunlight. Because the baby has been lying in a defecation-filled diaper for two hours, the mobile holds little appeal. There is no other human in the house right now except the baby, which the baby senses, crying loudly, fearfully. Just beyond the wall are the sounds of shooting and banging from a television program. These do not soothe. By the time a screen door slams, the baby squalls from such fear and loneliness that even the signal of a caregiver's approach is not enough to quiet the screams. The mother comes into the baby's room with kind comments at first, but then as the screaming baby flails in her arms, the mother becomes angry, throwing the child back in the crib. Shocked to an almost choking silence, the baby then resumes screaming from the crib bottom. The mother walks out of the room, slamming the door. She unloads her packages in the other room and turns the television on louder. Finally, she returns to the baby's room and changes the baby's dirty diaper. After completing this task, she leaves the screaming baby alone again in the crib.

This baby has experienced, in a few hours, the loneliness that is always so possible in a human lifetime—the unnatural lack of attachment between mother (or other primary caregiver) and baby, the child's terrible rise in internal stress, which in turn restricts the child's vision, security, and sense of the ubiquity of love and grace in the world. This baby needs certainty, not chaos, in order for the lamp of life to be well lit. But the baby does not have it—and the mother does not know how to attach to her child. The electromagnetic signals between caregiver and child are not refracting with clarity. When the baby squirms, the mother does not know to swaddle the little body tightly; she takes the squirming as a signal of rejection. When the baby wails, the mother becomes afraid of the child's fierce needs, and then she takes her own light, whose shine the baby yearns to feel, out of the room. The baby is left unable to experience either the light of self or the obvious light of the outside day refracted on the mobile, because the single most important light, at that moment, the electromagnetic relationship on which all else depends, has gone.

Human attachment is a journey of the soul. It is light apprehending signals of other lights. The development of the child is a development along endless patterns of light. Whether we observe a baby in a crib or by using a PET scan, noticing its myriad electrochemical cues; whether we watch a seven-year-old angry at his father; whether we visit a school for developmentally impaired students in Michigan, where elementary school students learn shapes and colors at a light table in order to enhance their learning; or we visit a juvenile mental hospital in California, where an ill teenager curls up in the corner that best refracts light from her window—no matter where we observe the soul of the child, we will notice what our religious forebears noticed: Light presents itself to us, waiting to be seen. And even further, light itself *develops*—it actually *grows*. The new sciences, especially neurobiology, have taught us this truth, which was originally suggested by ancient religions. Both religion and science show us the development of the soul of the child from birth to adulthood by following the light.

WATCH THE LIGHT GROW

Christianity teaches us: "As the child grows, so grows the breath and light of the Lord."

The Buddhist Lotus Sutras tell us: "The youth who grows to know himself brightens up the world like a moon set free from the clouds."

In the Hindu Upanishads we learn: "The child who grows to know himself is an ever-brightening jewel."

The Islamic Koran teaches: "Children grow in their parents' arms as if bathed in the light of God."

And in the Jewish Zohar: "As the child grows, so does the Light of God."

The commonality of these phrasings is quite beautiful, and all suggest that the daily and yearly *development* of the child is a journey of light. Given our understanding of the composition of the soul of the child, this should not surprise us. The new science of neurobiology can show us how beautifully and clearly this light develops the form of our children, echoing the fact that in all religious traditions, the soul of the child is seen as a journey of *staged, step-by-step* development called "the child." The light needs the child to exist, and the light needs the child to grow and adapt in order for the light itself to grow.

What does this mean?

THE SECRET LIFE OF A CHILD

According to astrophysicists, within you and your children is light-based particle residue of the big bang itself. When the Bible says, "From darkness came light," then says, "and God created Adam and Eve," physics and neurobiology combine to understand it this way: The original light, which cannot be destroyed, evolves in every human body *even at this moment.*

How beautiful, thus, to realize that the child in the crib is not only light, but also the original light of the universe. The internalized picture the well-attached mother has of her developing child, this child who is to her the most important piece of the universe, might be further seen by combined religion, physics, and neurobiology in these ways:

- Just as light, physically speaking, has no volume until it finds matter in which to evolve and reflect, the human soul needs the body in order to have volume.

- Just as light and matter are inseparable, so are the soul and body of the precious child inseparable.

- While light knows no time, matter knows time. Soul and body as one, developing as one, therefore experience both time and the timeless. Were there some world we could imagine in mythology or fantasy where the soul existed without the body—light without mass—then life as we know it would be nonexistent, because our bodies can exist only in time. However, the life we know, and the child development we nurture, is one of constantly growing electrobiological activity. And, as we care for our children, we are manipulating light, especially its speed.

Lijun Wang, a physicist at NEC Research Institute in Princeton, New Jersey, has used cesium gas to make light go faster than the 186,282 miles a second that we know as "the speed of light." In doing this he learned also about how light slows down. He learned that matter slows light down, alters the speed, and thus alters and changes the *experience* of light.

In the same way, we can understand our children's development and our role in it. Soul (light) and body (matter) are evolving together, unified, thus light gains experience, and matter gains existence. Existence and experience become one in the child. The child does not have the ability to see them as separate, as you and I do in writing and reading these sentences. The child in the crib is the original energy of the universe, whose electrobiological impulses move both at the speed of light and at the slowed-down pace of matter. The experience of timelessness the child has when a sudden insight occurs—"I'm being fed!"—like the experience of timelessness we adults have when we "suddenly see God" or "suddenly realize something extraordinary," is the best refraction of the speed of light of neurotransmission we will probably ever be conscious of. More commonly, 99.9 percent of our experiences—and of our child's—will be slower experiences of activity, relationship, and apprehension. They will not be less soulful for being slower activities, nor less enlightened.

In all this, neurobiology is shedding light on the somewhat mysterious path laid out by religion. We can better see now how the truths we hold dear are true, especially that who we are, and who we develop into being, is the light of God that needs to be embodied and nurtured in matter to be fully manifest. The sense we may have that not only do we need God, but that God needs us in order to be fully realized, can be seen in this idea (and we will develop it even further in Chapter 6). The soul is not merely a strand of energy we are born with that remains unchanged by our lives and then is emitted from us when we die. The soul grows as we grow. As the child smiles his or her individual smile, soul is growing.

THE HUMAN JOURNEY OF INDIVIDUALIZATION

Sigmund Freud recognized the light in the developing child when he said, somewhat angrily, "What a distressing contrast there is between the radiant intelligence of the child, and the feeble mentality of the average adult." We will not immerse ourselves so angrily in the development of child from infant to adult, but we will trace in these next few pages the wonder of the soul's development from birth to adulthood. It is the adults' care of the developing child that allows the individualization of the soul to happen.

In physical terms, we might think of it this way: Light-without-volume becomes an individual child of volume, weight, and mass—unique, special, and precious. In spiritual terms, God lives and develops as the developing soul of the individual child. It is very much up to us to determine the course of the light by how we *attach* to that light. Thus, as we explore the individualization of our children, we will also explore how human attachment works in the life of the developing human soul.

Stages of Individualization

When Freud lamented that the radiant intelligence of a child goes through growth stages that seem to darken the child into adulthood, he was pointing out (with a bad mood in tow) one of the ways we can observe the individualization of the light—the idea of children developing their individual identities in *stages*. This view of individualization provides a wonderful lens into your own child's development. Many thinkers and traditions worldwide have suggested that the soul develops in stages.

The ancient Hindus believed that the stages of individuality-development revolved around the seven chakras (energy and "light" points in the person):

1. anal

2. genital

3. solar plexus

4. heart

5. throat

6. third eye

7. crown

In the Hindu view, a child develops first an individual focus on grasping and possession (anal), then learns a sense of life as play (genital), then focuses on how to manage personal and social power (solar plexus), then moves to the search for romance and passion (heart), and so on through life. Not surprisingly, the anal phase is associated with early life, genital with early childhood, solar plexus with middle childhood, heart with early adulthood. The three remaining chakras continue through into later life.

Sigmund Freud, through purely personal insight or as a result of being influenced by ancient psychologies, developed a sequence for human psychological individualization in stages (growth of the *psyche*—soul in Greek) that uses some of the same terms as the Hindus—anal and genital—and adds some new ones, like latency. In our terms, we would say that Freud and the ancient Hindus were involved in defining how the soul itself actually grows in the child.

The Frenchman Jean Piaget, concerned more with cognitive than psychological development, presented four stages by which the individual psyche, or soul, grows:

- Sensorimotor (birth to two years). This is the development of the infant's and then toddler's brain from purely reactive behavior toward goal-oriented behavior.

- Preoperational (two to seven years). This includes the ability to understand symbols and use them to represent objects or ideas (like an alphabet).

- Concrete Operational (seven to eleven years). This includes the development of logic operations, as well as sophisticated physical operations.

- Formal operational (eleven years to adult). Now experimentation becomes systematic, and pure abstract thought is possible.

Lawrence Kholberg, an American, followed Freud and Piaget, developing a template for how the soul develops moral individualization—how children become moral individuals. For him there are six stages, each later stage including the previous stages. These six fit under an umbrella of three "levels" of individual moral development:

- The Preconventional Level (prior to about age six): Your child does things in response to rules that are set down by others in authority. The best way of guiding the child's character development at this level is to be a strong, sensitive authority.

- The Conventional Level (approximately ages six through twelve): Your child does things not only because adherence to rules is rewarded or punished but also because your child now understands duty and wants to be a good person for its own sake. The best way to guide a school-age child is by providing him or her with a clear sense of what is good, and involving the child in communities that support these values.

- The Postconventional (adolescence and beyond): Your child does things because his or her own ethical values—which have become fully individualized now and feel as if they have come completely from within—tell the young adult that he or she has acted well. The best way to guide this young adult is by having sophisticated talks and moral debates, by committing to public service and community work, and even by letting the child now become our moral teacher.

All these templates of individuality development, from whatever culture they come, provide standards of child behavior set for us by religious or secular observers of child development—standards by which we can determine whether our individual child is "growing up normally."

In the context of the soul of the child we are discussing in this book, we might see these standards not only in psychological or moral terms but also in spiritual terms, as the word *psyche* originally implied. We might notice that for each of these milestones or stages to be reached—whether genital, or concrete operational, or postconventional—the soul of the child must grow muscle, nerve cells, axons, dendrites, all using electrochemical neurotransmission. The soul of the child grows its light in a way templated in every human (for all humans, to a great extent, grow alike), but also in a unique way templated to the *individual* soul we name Gabrielle, Davita, David, or John.

We can watch the development of the stages of individualization—we can watch, in other words, the ever-brightening child—by noticing neurobiological growth patterns in the child we love. Just as we explored the science of the soul in the previous chapter, we can now explore the science of soul *growth*. This is a second major piece of the human and divine puzzle we are calling the soul of the child.

THE SCIENCE OF SOUL GROWTH

For clarity and brevity, I'm going to look with you at three general stages of soul growth and simply show how the individual light of the child is not static, but is growing and changing.

Stage 1: The First Three Years of Life

When your children were born, they had about half the neurons their adult brains will have. The second half developed at between six months and two years old. This is an early and simple way to watch the light of the child grow: The light doubles its volume in this time period. The quantity of neurons—of electric cells—in the brain is set by two years old. The quantity of *connections* is not set—maturity from two years old on will be very much about how the connections get made. But already in infancy we see that light is not static but grows—by millions of neurons—in the child. Genital phases, cognitive thinking, and moral competency all start in the neuronal growth of the infant brain.

As the child grows, not just light but also the vibrations in the brain that coincide with light-residues on PET scans, show increases both in volume and in frequency. What is so beautiful in all this is that both the volume and frequency of these light-vibrations grow *in direct relationship to attachment and bonding vibrations in the mother or other primary caregiver.*

Neuropsychiatrist Allan Schore has elucidated how this works: The primary caregiver of the child (let us say, here, the mother) *infuses* the child's internal electromagnetic energy. The child in turn infuses the mother via sympathetic vibrations of light—we call these "emotions"—as child and mother navigate their attachment.

Via PET scan, neurobiologists can actually watch the brain of the child light up when Mom comes in the room! The brain vibrates, light emissions increase, the body vibrates, signals, reaches out for Mom.

And from this interaction, the soul grows. Initially, the brain itself adds neurons; then, the mother (and others) helps the brain grow connectors. Then, even further, not only does the child's soul vibrate in relation to the mother, but its light is also actually *guided* by the mother's presence. We can watch the mother's vibratory resonance imitated by the child. The mother's light is guiding the child's. The child also begins, from very young, its individualization of that light by imitating the mother's (and others') light.

So we can observe soul growth through the addition of neurons, the increased electric vibration of neurons, and neurons being imitated; and we can see soul growth in another very clear way: the development of optical capacities—seeing and vision. At between two and four months, your child begins a neuroelectric growth spurt in the visual cortex that peaks at about eight months. By eight months, each neuron in the visual cortex connects to fifteen thousand other neurons. The soul of the child, genetically determined to access light, to see it and enjoy it, is not born with that capacity fully formed but must *develop* this capacity.

If there is immense growth of light capacity and manipulation in the visual cortex, we should also be able to see it in the other sensory cortices; if you could put a PET scan on your child's auditory or olfactory (hearing or smelling) cortex during this infancy period, you would not be disappointed. You would see light being multiplied by growth itself. If you could do the same with the limbic system, in the center of the brain, you would also notice amazing growth of light, especially as the top of the brain (the neocortex, where thought occurs) attaches to the limbic system (where emotions are shaped). This crucial pathway of electromagnetic light, like the visual cortex, is not set at birth. It must *grow*. It will grow no matter what, especially between ten and thirty-eight months, but the amount of light that grows and how good the connections are or how bad, depend to some degree on how the light around the infant operates. This is evidence yet again of not only light growing as it is templated by nature, but also of the *guidance* of the light—the laser beam quality of emotional development—by the mother, father, and others.

If, for instance, Mom, Dad, and others are attuned to the baby's expression of light—her smiles, his coos, her reaching out, his needs—the brain circuits between neocortex and limbic system grow more readily and more richly. If Dad repeatedly screams at the child, if Mom does not hold the child enough, those circuits grow less richly; the less rich the growth of light connections, the more likely the child is to experience less of the human emotional spectrum later in life—thus, less of the light spectrum. Studies by attachment specialist Daniel Stern, for instance, have shown that children whose caregivers did not match—via attunement to the child's signals—the child's natural, templated emotional state during the early years of life are far less likely to experience joy later in life.

Stage 2: Later Childhood

In glancing into the early years of life, we have focused on how light grows within the brain of the child, both with and without the help of caregivers. There is another way to watch soul growth: by observing older children engaged in physical activity—riding bikes, running, playing, walking together.

Galvanic skin response tests show us how the electrical energy of the child increases and thus actually *grows* during physical movement (and how it does not grow as richly when a child is a "couch potato"). When your child is enjoying the myriad and constant physical activities of seven-, eight-, or nine-year-olds, that little heart beats fast, pushing more blood and therefore more electricity through the system. Cells are excited, thus connecting to one another and growing. The brain receives more glucose and other nutrients, thus growing that "gray matter." Nerve connections become better lubricated by the advancing light.

The child, in a word, is more lit up. Children who do not exercise enough—who watch too much television or are not encouraged to "get out and play" by their parents—are, quite simply, less lit up than their more active peers. Their galvanic skin tests show less activity. Their PET scans show less brain activity. These children are more likely to be overweight. Eating disorders specialists have long claimed that overweight children are hiding, by their excess "armor," or body fat, "the real self" deep inside. This intuition is supported by neurobiology: The quantity of light in the child is actually decreased by a lack of exercise and by excessive weight. There is less lubrication and electrical growth. It is harder for the heart to work in this child, thus the heart excites fewer cells, the brain gets less glucose, and the nerve endings experience less variety.

To say that an obese child may not be as lit up as a child developing along the normal template is not to judge the value of either child; the obese child is no less an individual soul than any other. A neuroscientist is able to describe the quality of the experience of that soul, but not the value of that person. From the neurobiological point of view, the fact that an obese child is less lit up mainly says that there is a problem in diet, nutrition, and other habits and/or with the thyroid or another organ, that is not allowing the soul of the child to grow in the way it probably yearns to grow. Our children spend a great deal of time in physical activity or yearning for it; they are wise enough to realize—even if unconsciously and impulsively—that they need to move around in order to grow.

Our children also give us another wonderful indication of the human urge for soul growth. Right before our eyes, we notice our children actively imitating heroes and role models. In the same way that, during infancy, their vibrations were affected by Mom's, their brain growth now allows them to create internalized effects via people they don't even know.

At around eight years old, you may notice that your child starts modeling his or her individuality on Homer Simpson or Christina Aguilera. Your son may want to wear a Barry Bonds shirt. Your daughter may start singing Shania Twain songs, even following the body motions of the singer in concert. While most modeling of individuality comes from parents and those close to the child, the soul of the child is also directing energy toward identity and individuality models in the external environment. When we do a PET scan of an eight-year-old child, we notice bursts of light in the brain as the child goes through the Shania song, or verbalizes all the heroics Barry Bonds has accomplished in a season. The child is excited, and that excitement delights the child's cells.

Active identity modeling (dancing, talking, singing, playing), just like attachment to caregivers, and even reading, excites the child's brain; this should not surprise us. As a growing light, the soul is activated both by the real (multisensory-emotive-intellectual experience) and the virtual (limited sensory-emotive-intellectual experience), and more by someone in person to talk to or dance with or sing in front of than by a passive stimulant like a video game. When we use a PET scan on children reading, we notice far more of their brain lighting up than when they are watching a typical "kids program" on TV. Even reading creates more access to the real—because it requires active use of the imagination—than does television, which does so much of the imaginative work for the soul that it allows for passivity. When a child watches Shania Twain on TV less of the brain lights up than when she sings and dances like Shania Twain.

No matter how your child has spent the time between the early years and late childhood, whether as a couch potato, or as a very active school-age child, a process of renovation occurs in the brain beginning at about ten years old. This process is further evidence of how the soul grows. But the house of self is not razed during this time. It's more like this: A lot of the furniture and many of the walls inside the self get replaced. We might say—in the context of light development—that the locations of lamps and overhead lights shining in the house can, by about twelve, change. These new changes will last into adolescence.

This renovation process is called "pruning" by neurobiologists. Nerve cells that have been used—for instance, if your child plays soccer regularly—continue to be used; but those that have not—for instance the brain has cells for music, but let's say your child does nothing musical during these years—tend to get pruned away.

Areas in the frontal lobe, which are especially crucial for judgment, insight, and planning, can get pruned away, so if your child is not prodded to develop good judgment, plan out time, and seek insight into both commonplace and mysterious things, neurotransmission may not be guided or "lasered" toward these activities, activities which are, arguably, some of the most important in your child's development of individuality and maturity.

While the child's brain is pruning, the body will begin secreting adolescent doses of hormones. This hormonal stimulation in the child, which shepherds in adolescence, often alerts us to how the cells of not only the brain but also the body are being renovated. Nutrition becomes very important. It has always been important, but as we move toward adolescence, toward the rivers of light-cells called hormones, foods and beverages taken in by the child's body are even more immediately processed as neuroelectric stimulants and depressants.

When children eat junk food, their neuroprocessing is deeply affected. When a ten- or eleven-year-old eats junk food it is likely that the food will—if the child has "fat" genes, for instance—actually change the child's body right before our eyes. It is not melodramatic to say that the light of the child is darkened by bad nutrition. We now have the technology to watch food processing in the stomach, nervous system, and brain. With this technology, we notice the heaviness of cells caused by high-fat, high-carbohydrate foods, like french fries, fast-food hamburgers, and soda pop.

In the developing body of the child, this darkening of cells—this alteration of amino acids and the distortion of normal serotonin secretions—leads to problems such as eating disorders, needless dieting, athletic and learning problems, mood and behavior problems, and mental illness. What a child eats affects the soul of that child. Often it is obvious in our children's sudden behavior changes or gradual weight gain, but we do nothing. Then, before you know it, adolescence is upon us. Hormones, which are fast-moving cells of light, begin to rule the growth of the soul as never before.

Stage 3: Adolescence

The neurology of the human brain restructures itself during adolescence, triggered by the flood into the brain of neuroelectric circuitry known as hormones. Hormones are highly charged, highly electrified neural cells that stimulate the growing brain to repattern itself toward adulthood: thus, grew the soul toward individuality.

One amazing fact we've recently learned: At least half the neural connections in the prefrontal cortex—which is like the air traffic controller of a person's brain—are obliterated by hormonal intrusion for a period of time (sometimes months, even years) during adolescence. Decision making in the brain relies, for this time of transition, on greater input from the limbic system and other parts of the brain that handle emotional reactions. So when you notice adolescents taking extra risks, making "bad decisions," getting into addictions, and being overly emotional, you are noticing this obliteration in the prefrontal cortex. The brain does, after transition, regain new, full circuitry, and the adult decision maker shows through. But we have to be vigilant guides during this time period, providing clear supervision, limits, and expectations. Our children intuit that their light, as growing adolescents, is adjusting to ever-new and confusing social qualities of shadow and experience. As we supervise and guide adolescents, we help direct their light into the laser beam, helping them avoid the chaotic emotional reactions that can be part of an unsupervised adolescent life.

One of the last developmental steps of the child's soul is the myelination of cells in the brain. At around twenty years old (for some a little earlier, for some a little later—girls earlier than boys), the brain completes its electrochemical development of the gooey white substance that quickens every transmission and coats, protects, and even hardens the brain during adulthood. That the brain completes brain growth does not mean that the light of your child will not change during life—our brain cells and our bodies continue growing throughout life. But adult growth and child/adolescent growth are not the same. Adult growth—brain growth after full myelination—is slower than adolescent and child growth.

In this rendering of some of the key elements of brain and body activity during child development, I hope you've seen how the soul's light grows. Saint Augustine wrote, "The soul is the light of the body." While he, locked in a previous age, only knew the soul as unchanging light *borrowed* by the body, we can now see how the light actually *grows* as body in a human lifetime. The human soul is changed by this life. We have the amazing scientific ability, and with it new intuitions, to see that the human soul, God in the child, is not static—but actually grows like a flower.

FLOWERING

The Buddhists use the beautiful term "flowering" for the growth of the soul. They conceive of the soul as "flowering" right before our eyes. This is somewhat like a parent saying, "My daughter has really started to flower this year." Or: "My son's talents are really coming to fruition." These phrases indicate the sweet display of the child's soul in everyday life. Christians warn against sinning. Hindus warn children to act well or there will be consequences in future lives. These religions know that the flowering of the soul—even in "the afterlife" or future lives—is deeply affected by what it does here and now.

The soul flowers in infancy, as the number of neurons in the

brain doubles between birth and two years old. It flowers in childhood, as the brain and body learn to navigate the world. It flowers
during the brain-cell pruning period, between childhood and adolescence. It flowers as the frontal lobes develop in our teens. It flowers as the brain finishes developing myelin in our early twenties. It
flowers in these ways we've noted just above, and in a million other
ways.

The soul does not grow or flower in a vacuum, of course.
Some of soul growth is patterned or templated genetically at birth
(the topic of our next chapter). Because of our basic human tem-
plating, even if a child is brought up in a cave and not taught language before adulthood, some language skills can still be learned
in adulthood because the human brain is templated, genetically,
to self-generate tissue in the language centers of the left hemisphere.

On the other hand, if a child is taught language from early on,
tissue in those brain centers grows better because constant neurotransmission—activity of light—among those neurons occurs, stimulated by the environment (the parent talking to the child).
Children whose parents read to them in the first two years of life
become better readers on average than children whose parents do
not because the activity of reading—a form of human attachment—stimulates brain growth. The child whose parents didn't
read aloud will most probably still learn to read, but with a greater
likelihood of reading less well than a peer child whose parents did
read aloud.

In all this we are, of course, saying that in order to flower, the
soul needs help. As we have been hinting throughout this chapter,
the light of the child needs what is called *attachment*. Without
attachment, the soul grows with greater emotional stress. We could

say that light and shadow in the soul become chaotic, not happily ordered. In biological terms, cortisol (stress hormone) levels rise, releasing clotting elements in the blood that depress the immune system; cholesterol levels rise, muscles tense, blood pressure rises, other hormones and brain chemicals—like serotonin, which makes us feel good—lessen. The light grows less well.

The child who was well cared for in the crib and human community lived in a world where electromagnetic signals between individual child and caregivers were so healthy and understood that the soul of the child and the soul of the adult were one. Attachment specialist Louise Kaplan calls this secure attachment *oneness*. The child and adult do not feel disconnected. Their individualities are intertwined in Oneness.

Think of the flower, which appears to be separate from the soil and even the stem, but is not separate. It is completely interwoven into the world of light represented by sun, water, soil, and photosynthesis. In the same way, a child is not separate. Separation is a psychological concept—that is, a child "separates" from his mother in order to grow up. In spiritual terms, however, the child is flowering in concert with all caregiving. It is specifically when the child loses clear access to the symbiosis of soil, nutrients, and sun that he or she will wither. The flower needs all the elements of light—from oxygen to photoelectricity—in order to flourish.

It is the same with human beings. When children who are flowering—becoming individuals—lose the attention of those they love, they wither. Neurobiology, which is the science of soul growth, has shown us this.

SOUL GROWTH, STRESS, AND CORTISOL

A child who generally lacks access to love and attention also experiences (1) greater risk of damage to the templated brain development path, and (2) compensatory though dangerous neural growth. The soul's growth, the light of that child, is harshly affected, as would be the light of a child who is physically, psychologically, or sexually abused, or who suffers from other family trauma, or from ongoing attacks on the soul by media, lack of security, oppressive poverty, racism, sexism, or any other prolonged attack on the psyche.

Amazingly, we can now actually watch the light of the child be affected by these stresses. We can see it on PET scans and read it off of stress hormone indicators. Children who are under significant and constant emotional stress show impeded light activity on PET scans. In other words, where a normal child would show light activity of neurons firing, the chronically stressed child shows dark spots, or "gaps," on the brain. After a period of months, those dark spots do not change. Adequate brain development does not occur there. That child's brain has been altered by stress. A severely abused child, if a male, is more likely to grow up to be a sexual predator; if a female, she is more likely to develop an eating disorder. The darkness on the brain is the electrobiological result of raised cortisol levels.

Children who are under significant emotional stress show consistently higher cortisol levels than normal children and experience very real brain pattern changes. The longer the cortisol level is at peak quantity, the greater the effect on brain patterning. Not only do low cortisol levels lead to a feeling of being secure and high cortisol levels lead to feelings of insecurity and despair, but the longer a child experiences the stress of abuse, the longer the heightened cortisol levels last, the more consistently we notice that the growth of the amygdala—which regulates feeling and aggression—is affected. There is less light there, thus less ability to regulate feeling and aggression. We also notice that less light moves from the limbic system, where emotions are parsed out, to the parts of the temporal and frontal lobes that help the child act morally. We notice similar brain pattern differences in light on PET scans of children who develop borderline and narcissistic personality disorders.

According to some estimates, these personality disorders are suffered by up to twenty million young adults. They begin with attachment stress in the first three years of life (and continue to develop during later developmental trauma). Right-hemisphere brain development is especially affected by a lack of secure attachment in the first three years of life. Neurobiologists have learned that the developing brain of the child depends on what is called "affect synchrony" between caregiver—usually the mother along with a very close second mother (like devoted grandma, intimate father, or consistent and long-term child care provider)—and the child. When the mother is present and well attached, affect synchrony exists—the soul of the child flowers beautifully under the mother's light. It synchronizes its affect with the mother's caregiving affect. If, however, the mother is not present and attached, the child will have more difficulty with synchrony—cortisol levels will rise, and right-hemisphere development is impeded.

It should come as no surprise to us, given what we've learned so far, that the best way to notice if affect synchrony exists is to watch the light in the eyes of a child. As neurobiologist Allan Schore has put it: "When mutual eye contact is established, both [mother and child] know that the loop between them has been closed, and this is the most potent of all social situations." For the growing soul, the light of attachment is the most powerful light in the baby's universe.

A Culture of Cortisol

Many neurobiologists believe that our human developmental cortisol levels are higher now—despite the fact that we live in an age of relative material luxury—than they were one hundred years ago, when many more of our ancestors scraped together a living. When we compare cortisol levels of poor people in India with cortisol levels of middle-class Americans, we can see an interesting, though not yet conclusive, difference. Cortisol levels among many middle-class American children are *higher* than those of many poor children in India. These findings bring home the fact that the flowering of the child's soul might have more to do with attachment to caregivers than with material wealth. The Indian children, though poor, are brought up in richly layered extended families. The American children are often raised in broken families or nuclear families that do not get much help from their extended families.

Neurobiologists like Daniel Amen have long been making the case that children in the Western world are under more chronic emotional stress today than we realize. The attachment systems that provide soil and nutrients for the soul are breaking down. Mothers are gone from children during the early years of life, and caregivers (like day care providers) are not Grandma or Auntie. These caregivers are paid so little, many must quit their jobs (and thus their attachment to our infants) frequently—so they don't attach as well to our children as a mother, grandma, or auntie might. In the late childhood and early adolescent periods, our fathers, grandfathers, and other elder men are especially absent from the attachments necessary to guide and direct the light of adolescent development. Parents, extended families, and children spend less time together today than a hundred years ago, even though we all know that the family is the "building block of a society." Our children seem lonelier for the soil and sun from which they came than any previous generation has been.

In this we find the hyperindividualization of children—an overemphasis on the independence of the child and de-emphasis on parenting, supervision, and guidance. It would not be so severe a risk for children and society if our children's brains were formatted to handle it. But we live in a hyperstressful time with brains that, as neuroscientist Robert Sylwester has pointed out, were actually formatted for life thousands of years ago. Modern life moves too fast for a lot of our children's brains, and our children suffer a disease too rarely discussed: *overstimulation*. Not only abuse and neglect but also overstimulation directly increase cortisol levels, thus soul growth. Educator Robert Kegan uses the phrase "in over our heads" to describe today's young people. They are literally in over their heads, neurally. It is no wonder that rates of brain disorders among children have skyrocketed in the last three decades. Millions now suffer from attention deficit disorder, attention deficit hyperactive disorder, dyslexia, bulimia, anorexia, and depression.

Unfortunately, at the very time in human evolution when our children's brains are highly overstressed, their lives are lived in diminished attachment. These two factors together are dangerous to the growing soul—the flowering—of the child. The danger shows up well—though we often miss it—in misfirings of the very fragile, developing human brain.

PROTECTING THE LIGHT

"Light coherence" is what physicists call *the attachment of light to light*. This is a term useful to soul growth as well. While we would probably all agree that human individuality is a primary value of the modern world, and while we might all also agree that the goal of individualization itself is for a child to become a free adult individual, we have missed the fact that light loves light, light needs light, light is attracted to and attaches to light. We can certainly split an atom, thus splitting its electrical field in two (or a thousand); but in its natural state, that atom wants to be a cohesion of protons, electrons, neurons. The human brain and body feel best in a well-ordered coherence of light cells and activity.

We notice light coherence when we think of families, attachment systems, day cares, and neighborhoods. They work well, allowing the best grace of individualization, when they protect and secure the soul of the child. When individualization runs amok, without supervision; when every child goes his or her own way; when there is chaos and splitting, light does not cohere. There is violence, abuse, neglect, aggression, and just plain trouble. Ironically, individual freedom is not protected in this scenario. When the safety and security of the soul are not protected, freedom withers.

This is the situation we face today, as we seek to manage the soul growth of our children. Overstimulation, abuse, broken attachments, and the other forms of cortisol-raising stimulation are affecting child development. Sadly, no matter how sensitized our population gets to this generation's heightened mental illness and brain disorder statistics (to be discussed further in Chapter 6), many still insist this is all an illusion—a trick of light.

"Maybe all these terrible things in children's lives existed at these rates a hundred years ago but we just didn't notice them back then." This idea has been tossed about by well-meaning people, but it is unsupported by any government or independent research. Some five million children have ADD or ADHD; some ten million suffer depression. We have no reason to believe it was ever this way before, and certainly no proof.

A Cure for Cortisol—The Extended Family

Not surprisingly, one fact is corroborated in every psychological study: cortisol levels decrease, and brain and psychological disorders show up less frequently and are best controlled, when children have a secure attachment not just to one, but also to a *group* of caregivers whose love and attention are unwavering *throughout the stages of soul growth.*

In *The Wonder of Girls,* I presented to readers *The Anne Frank Principle.* Anne Frank's life story provides an example of how important extended family is: how a group of people can protect soul growth over a long developmental period. Though Anne Frank, who hid from the Nazis in a secret annex with her extended family for two years, grew up under immense external stress, she still flowered. She lived a life true to her individual emotional and spiritual nature *because she grew up in the arms of the many people with whom she was intimately bonded.*

The importance of more than one caregiver cannot be overestimated in our era. Cortisol levels among children of single parents is, on average, statistically higher than stress hormone levels among children with two parents, or with strong extended families. Also, one of the leading causes of increased cortisol levels in children is divorce.

This does not mean a single parent can't do a great job caring for the soul she or he loves. It does mean, however, that the job is much harder; it also means that it is ever more important, from the base viewpoint of the growing soul, that we protect family stability and build and rebuild extended families (the subject of Chapter 6).

I hope that by showing you in this chapter how the light in your child's eyes actually grows, and noting how it can be altered by your attachment, I am inspiring you to move toward a new viewpoint about your relationship to your child. We will continue developing this viewpoint in the next chapter, which is about knowing ourselves in divine relationship with children. We are not merely parents and our children merely kids—we are all, through the fact of our relationship, holy.

THE PRECIOUS CHILD

"That girl came out of the womb with her own personality," we say, laughing. "That kid came out all boy," we say, and then chuckle, "but also a unique individual." From early on, we know the light of the universe in our individual child, and we sense that our job is to help our child "become a worthy individual in the world." The Original Light Source—which we sometimes call God or Brahman—has chosen our child in whom to be realized, and our child is an individual form of the Light. When we feel the immense joy of our child's birth—our electromagnetic, joyful pulsing of our heart rate, brain waves, hormones—we realize, in an instant, how much our child is the light of God. Over the months and years, we "raise our child to be an adult," often forgetting that initial speed-of-light realization we felt, that sudden sense of the infinite source.

Our child individualizes, becomes "so much herself," "so much himself," "so completely David," "so completely Jennifer," and we get bogged down in parenting, overwhelmed by the daily grind; we may forget that the *soul* of our child is developing in our arms, our homes, our schools, our neighborhoods.

The new sciences give us a way to remember. I hope in this chapter you have gotten a sense of how the light your child is not only light itself, but *grows* as light. In the next chapter, we will explore through the new genetic sciences the map—often unseen by us until we shed just the right light upon it—that each of our children is born with. The map we are talking about has been called "marks on the soul" by aboriginal religions, "an individual's destiny" by Western thinkers, "genetic coding" by scientists. It is an amazing map indeed, and your child was born because of it.

3

SOUL MARKINGS: THE DIVINE MAP A CHILD IS BORN WITH

To realize one's destiny is a person's only obligation.

—PAULO COELHO

The sun shone that afternoon as I parked the car at the hospital. About forty-eight hours before, my friend Ruby with husband, Jim, at her side, had given birth by C-section to their first child, Lindsey, two and a half months premature. Leaving my car and taking the elevator up to the preemie wing, I knew Mom was healthy but worried about the baby. Six and a half months is very young for birth into this life.

At the nurses' station, Carla, a jovial RN with a broad smile and efficient eyes, guided me to a nursery window, where she showed me tiny Lindsey. The first child of my friends Jim and Ruby, Lindsey lay beyond the window in a glass case, connected to electrical monitors and oxygen tubes. My throat filled with emotion, my eyes watered, and my hands trembled as I watched this one-pound-eight-ounce girl struggle to keep the light in her body.

"She's already got a definite personality," Carla said, smiling and placing her hand on my shoulder to comfort me.

"It's hard to see her this way," I murmured. She was more a shriveled mass than a child, her eyes not open, her fist-size chest heaving from the force of mechanical oxygen, her pulse barely visible on the monitor, a tiny intravenous tube shoved into her needle-thin, purplish arm.

Carla agreed but said, "She's gonna make it, and she's gonna be a spunky kid. You mark my words. I've seen all kinds of preemies. Lindsey's got something in her some of them don't. She's gonna come through just fine."

This was very good to hear, and I thanked Carla for her words, which perhaps she spoke to anyone who seemed saddened by the powerlessness of watching a premature baby hanging on to life. Carla went back to her work, and I went down the hall toward Jim and Ruby's room. I found Ruby sleeping, and Jim sitting back in a chair, watching a ball game, without the volume. Upon seeing me at the door, he stood then stepped out into the hall and moved with me back to where his baby was, reporting everything that was being done for her. He said more than once, "All the doctors and nurses are saying she's got a lot going for her. Her pulse is steady, brain-wave patterns are normal for this age. They might keep her a month in here, but she should make it."

Jim, who appeared all cried out over the last twenty-four hours, leaned on the glass, gazing at his child. "The nurse, Carla, says she sees something strong in Lindsey already," I reported.

Jim nodded. "It's amazing. Each of these preemies is a little different. They look the same but they're all unique. I guess Lindsey's a little spunkier than some." There was Carla's word, *spunky*.

"It's going to be all right," I said.

"We live on hope and prayer," Jim confessed. "We just have to hope she's got life enough in her to make it. Pray for us, will you?" he pleaded.

I confirmed with him that I would.

Lindsey is now three years old. She is a nearly normal child— she does suffer from more bronchial infections than normal, but her brain and body are developing normally. I made four visits to the preemie wing to see Lindsey after her birth. During my last, I asked Carla how many babies born at six months make it to normal. She said, "Very few." But Lindsey, as Carla had intuited early on, had "spunk."

Jim is a microbiologist and geneticist. When Ruby's pregnancy had begun to develop problems, he'd confessed how powerless he felt. "I know so much about the body," he said to me, "but there's only so much anyone can do." This seemed strangely unlike Jim, who always had an answer to every puzzle of the human organism. I asked him what he or Ruby could do, and he said, "We're doing what we have to—bed rest, dietary changes, keeping stress very low. These will help, but probably the most important thing is our genes. Our baby should have good genetic markers for physical health. This may get her through."

Jim and Ruby are marathon runners. They rarely get sick. They come from very healthy families, with good longevity. They have a very positive attitude about life; neither of them is a very anxious person. These were the genetic markers he primarily meant.

We've talked, now that Lindsey is growing up, about what got her through. Jim often returns to the genes, his life work.

"We now know," he tells me, "that there's a genetic marker for just about everything."

"Is there a genetic marker for 'spunkiness'?" I asked him.

"Most assuredly," he replied.

Jim, a friend and supporter of my work, has taken me to his genetics lab. It is the place that gives him his professional sustenance, and also his personal feeling of powerlessness. It is a place where any of us, if we look and listen carefully, can notice the divine ardor of the universe, in which revelations are possible through both religion and science; and yet it is a place where mystery remains.

"With each new thing we discover," Jim told me on one of our visits, "we realize how absolutely beautiful life is, and how mysterious."

"What remains a mystery?" I joked. "You've charted the genome, right? What's left?"

"The 'why' is still the mystery," he said with his usual seriousness. "But you're right, the genetic markers are not so mysterious anymore."

Jim's lab—which he shares with other scientists, graduate students, and computer technicians—is like a small warehouse. It's an open space, with painted white walls and mainly white or metallic furniture (lab tables, regular tables, cabinets, chairs). The colorful exceptions exist in the computer areas, where data from colorful laser studies are analyzed.

"One day it'll all fit on a CD-ROM," Jim told me, pointing to the whole lab and all its apparatus. "Everything we need to know will fit right in our hands."

Jim took me to an area where he "shreds" DNA. Very fine lasers cut DNA strands into two or three thousand nucleotides.

Lasers also read DNA strands that are extracted and dyed. The fluorescent DNA fragments, fed into sequencing tubes, are hooked up to computers. These computers look for DNA fragments that intersect with one another. Upon finding them, computer images show scientists the billionth of the genome being mapped.

I noticed aloud with Jim how dependent everything in his lab seemed to be on light—lasers, microscopes, computer imagery, all existing because there is light.

He agreed.

"It's almost as if the genome is a little spark of light," I said, wondering how he'd respond.

"It's probably the original spark of the universe inside each of us," Jim said. "The genome is God hidden in everyone." I've never known Jim to be a highly religious man, so I did not pursue any religion/science connections with him. But inwardly, I celebrated his remark. It seemed to fit so well with what all of our ancestors believed and expressed through religious language; it fit with the direction of my own thinking and primal, even if unconscious, memories we all have.

Jim continued my tour, especially now that I'd gotten him on the subject of how light was used to discover the contours of the minuscule light at the heart of being. He showed me how fluorescence is added to molecules, how these molecules are put on glass chips, how lasers read the genes; then he talked about how disease-causing genes can be discovered through this method. They are lit up. He mentioned a colleague in Europe who had discovered a breast cancer gene, another a language gene.

When Jim and I went to lunch in the cafeteria, I asked him

about cloning. I was especially curious about how light and light molecules fit into that kind of genetic engineering.

"Are you kidding?" He smiled. "It's all about light. All molecules themselves are light."

"Okay," I agreed. "Fair enough. How about cloning? How is light used in cloning? Is it like in your lab?"

"The process is like fusion," he explained. "Fission, of course, is where you split the atom. Fusion, on the other hand, is usually thought of as the opposite (though that's too simplistic). But it's really the use of one light source to manipulate and fuse two others. The nucleus of a donor egg is taken out, and that's fused with a cell from the sheep or, one day, the person you're trying to copy. The whole process is done by using lasers and light. If that's what you're after."

I nodded. "I'm interested in the connection between light and life itself. Tell me what makes the new fused cell grow?" I asked. "It's put together via light, but is it like a plant? Does it flower because of something like the sun? Or is it like Lindsey, in the preemie ward? Is it oxygen?"

"Well," he replied, "Lindsey, of course, grew because of a panoply of factors—oxygen, IV nutrients, and so on."

"Which are all based in light, since they're molecular, right?"

"Sure."

"And that's what makes the clone grow?"

"Yes," he said. "Electrical current is the source of growth for all cells. The electrical current makes the reconstituted, or 'cloned,' cell grow into a duplicate. The microbiologist has equipment like mine that invests the reconstituted cell with electricity."

"The cell can't duplicate without electrical current?" I asked.

"Not possible," he replied.

And so there it was again. Electricity, light, the soul—hints of God. When the first cell was created in this universe, electrical current, light at light speed, seems to have created it. If our religious imaginations needed verifying, the labs of geneticists and microbiologists seem to provide verification: As humans now create new humans, we too rely on electromagnetic currents—on light.

When Jim and I finished our visit that day, I asked after his family, Lindsey especially. She was doing well. Later that week, I visited Jim and Ruby. Indeed, she seemed quite normal, though she did cough from a mild bronchial infection. "I'm working on that," Jim assured me. "By the time she's ten, I hope to know how to use stem cells to cure her."

"Is it fair to say," I asked Jim, "that you are decoding the map your child was born with? You as a scientist see a map in her, and you can read it?"

"Absolutely!" he agreed, liking the image. "That's a great way to put it. I'm an explorer following a map—I'm looking for a treasure hidden in a cave. I'll find it and it'll be her cure."

"If you were prone to use religious language," I challenged him, "would you call it 'a map of the soul'?"

"If I were prone that way," he said, nodding. "Paul Davies, the physicist, says, 'We human beings are built into the great scheme of things in a very basic way.' That is certainly true. The genome is an example of what he means. I'd say, if there's a 'soul,' its original map would be our genome. I hope there is a soul." Jim smiled. "I'd love to think we're mapping it."

"Oh, there's a soul," Ruby said, scooping up her daughter and bringing her over to us. "Look at our Lindsey." Ruby hugged her daughter, whom she had almost lost so many times in those early months of life. Drawing her close, Ruby held her daughter in a way that reminded me of early Renaissance paintings in which Mary is holding the baby Jesus still for a second, as if the painter could take a photograph.

Then Lindsey wrestled free, moving into her father's arms.

"Every child is divine," I said, smiling, prompted perhaps by the ancient image in my mind.

"Especially mine!" Jim laughed, cuddling Lindsey.

And so I said my good-byes to this kind family, thinking, Is that not a statement all parents have felt in their bones? Not only that children are divine, but that especially *mine* is divine. How deep the genetic connection is between parent and child!

What if the new sciences we've discussed, when combined with the field of genetics, are now showing us why we have that intuitive, blood-and-bone feeling? What if this new science is going deep into the map of the soul each child contains, offering revelations about the divinity of the child, and the divine marks on the child's soul?

These issues are the subject of this chapter. When we hold our children, or help doctors keep children alive, or watch scientists like Jim work with genetic markers, we are witnessing the science of the divine child right before our eyes.

THE DIVINE CHILD

Though the terms "genetic markers" and "genetic blueprint" sound new, born of contemporary science, they have old roots. The ancient Hindus, for instance, began a process of medicine called

Ayurveda, which is founded on the understanding that each individual has a unique "mind-body blueprint" by which he or she can be known. To the Hindus, this blueprint is, in pure form, the divine map itself. An individual is a unique combination of three categories of divine markers: *vatta, pitta, kapha.* In Ayurvedic medical theory, disease or sickness comes as a result of an individual's forgetfulness of the internal and divine map. He or she neglects the personal blueprint, thus neglecting to stay in sync with the natural workings of the universe.

In the religions of aboriginal peoples "soul markings" is the phrase used for the map within the child. The Huichol of ancient Mexico, for instance, talk of "marks on the soul." The ancient shamans of Russia talk of "those marks on the soul that guide the life of the baby to adulthood." These shamans go further, saying that rites of passage during adolescence should be linked, for greatest effectiveness, to the "marks on the soul" that parents and elders see in the child upon birth.

Australian aborigines link soul markings to rites of passage as well, saving some of the soil from the spot at which a girl's birth took place in order to mix it with her first menstrual blood.

These "primitive" practices point to the importance of *birthright* among our long-ago ancestors, who lived closer to the basics of human development: An individual was the son or daughter of a whole tribe that stretched back through the ages, and his or her soul was marked by "ancestors," bloodlines, and lineage.

In this philosophy, which was accepted by all of our original peoples—whether from Europe, Africa, Asia, or elsewhere—the child is a *divine* child, connected to God through ancestry and soul markings. What God wanted of an individual child could be read—by parents, grandparents, and shamans—in the eyes, body, and personality—the light—of the child. *Every* child was "special" in this way—not just the children of those who were rich, royal, or religious.

As human population increased, this idea of the "divine child" became an idea very much reserved for the children of kings (mainly the male children), and the prophets. King David was known as a divine child, linked directly to God. Kings Henry, Richard, and John, as well as Queen Elizabeth of Shakespeare's time, were known as divine children, their reigns blessed by God because they were direct descendants of the holy, royal family. Religious prophets were known as divine children. Jesus' divinity is established by Mary's still being a virgin at his birth. Not Joseph, a mortal, but God, the divine immortal, impregnated Mary with the holy child. Christianity borrowed this from Greek mythology. When Zeus, the highest Greek god, impregnated mortal women, like Leda, their progeny were immediately considered divine. Without Zeus's parentage, they were "only mortal." In depicting Jesus this same way, the early Christians absorbed the best of the Greek and Roman religions into the new religion, Christianity.

While humanity made the journey of ideas from "every child is a divine child, directly linked to Mother Earth and Father Sky" to "only royal and prophetic children are divine children, directly linked to God," an evolving humanity also made the long journey to modern civilization. The human population had been rising during this five-thousand-year period by the millions, then, more recently, by the billions. Throughout this cataclysmic change, it helped all of our ancestors to think that a few people were divine children, their souls marked by God for leadership. It helped because the divinity of the many could be transferred, thus, onto the divinity of the one person, and the many would thus allow themselves to be organized by that one person to whom they entrusted their life force. This led to an order much needed in the face of population growth that changed everything about human life and stressed available resources. It appeared, for a long time, that the only way to control people was to keep divine rights for the few.

Beginning with the Enlightenment, and with the democratic and egalitarian movements that ensued, humanity began to develop a new sense: that even in high-population cultures, each human should again be considered the divine child with an inherent, equal birthright. The American Declaration of Independence, with its assurance that we have "certain unalienable Rights, [and] among these are Life, Liberty and the pursuit of Happiness," represented the idea that each of us is equal, and because these rights came from God, each of us had direct access to the divine force that marked us with these rights. The Enlightenment was not called the En*light*enment for nothing.

Now here we are, in the midst of two decades of amazing new science, able to recognize the democratic idea (one that actually harkens back to ancient times) that each of us is a soul marked by eternity. The science of genetics is our aid in this. It also helps us go further than our ancestors, for now we can develop a clear understanding of what many of the child's divine markings are, how they work, how we can nurture them, and what happens to our children if we do not.

GENETICS: SOUL MARKINGS

The ancient Jewish Cabalists said that God, or Light, gets a chance to individualize through us. God, a Mass of Light, has no volume, thus needs matter to give it form, so God is formless unless embodied. The Cabalists further point out that at the time of the explosion, when Sound and Light became individual slivers, these individual slivers carried the markings of the original Sound and Light, that are passed on to this day.

Jewish geneticists decided, about a decade ago, to see if they could prove just a portion of this idea. Among the Jews are three kinds of people—Kohainim, Levitim, Israelitim—the "Kohain," the "Levites," and the "Israelites." Most Jews are Israelites. Descendants of the next group in the hierarchy, who hold some of the important religious jobs, are the Levites. And the descendants of the original priests of the Old Testament are the Kohain. Jewish geneticists decided to discover if there was a genetic way of determining which Jews were which. In studying African Kohainim they isolated a marker on the human chromosome that indicated Kohain descendancy. They asked for samples from Kohainim (and controls from the other two groups) around the world. This new study verified their early finding: *there is a chromosome marker for Kohainim.* Studies are under way regarding Levites and Israelites right now.

This Kohain chromosome study is just one example of how the new science of genetics is discovering markers on the souls of our children, and therefore, in each of us. The mapping of the genome, in which Jim was so invested, is the overarching umbrella under which these other studies take place. Should it come as any surprise to us that the primary tool used to study genetics, the genome, and genetic markers is *light?* When I toured Jim's genetics lab, I could not miss how the concentration of light—through high-powered microscopes and computer imaging—makes possible the study of the soul and God. Light, we might say, knows light.

These new human abilities to understand and cohere light have discovered certain basic elements of soul that you and your child are. We now know:

- There is a "code of codes," as my friend Jim calls it, or "the blueprint of human life," as molecular biologist Greg Schuler calls it; it possesses 3.2 billion chemical markers—known as "letters" (each letter represents a molecule such as adenine, cytosine, or thymine). This blueprint, called "the human genome" by scientists like Jim, Schuler, Karl Stefannson, and William Haseltine of the worldwide human genome project, is our human heritage and birthright.

- Each individual person—you, me, your child—contains the map, the human genome, in an individualized sequence; thus the general birthright, the general mass, is individualized in our unique personal sequencing.

- Every cell in your child contains a copy of the genome he or she is born with; you and your child do not have any cells that don't include the "blueprint of human life." Each of us is unique, but we are also *completely contained in the whole.*

- Our individual closeness to the whole can now be tracked: Humans have eighty-thousand genes, 99.9

percent of which are *identical.* Thus, your child and your neighbors differ from one another in only one of a thousand chemical letters.

- Each human gene achieves its aims by fusing light: Each gene is actually a protein code, in letter triplets, which directs the cell toward the amino acids in the human system to fuse with. This fusing is what makes life happen in your child's body.

- The human genetic constitution we are describing has changed little despite the advent of farming, industry, medical science, and even technology. Changes obvious to us—we do not walk on four legs anymore—are small changes when taken against the monolithic backdrop of the whole genetic code.

- Each human brain involves a unique sequencing of genes, with each gene—like "the short gene," which is found in people who are anxious and worry—coding neurotransmission to accomplish specific tasks in the neural web. In other words, the speed-of-light transmission of information in the brain is far more genetically programmed than we've realized, and many of our expressions of self—from depression to aggression—are written on the genome we are individually born with.

- Studies of twins raised completely apart have externally corroborated the findings geneticists have made by studying DNA itself. In one study, for instance, at the University of Minnesota, twins who were raised apart were very similar to each other (despite being raised very differently, by very different parents, in very different environments), even down to being equally "conventional," "enterprising," and "artistic," and even sharing similar interests, like baking, science, or public speaking. Identical twins, not surprisingly, were even more likely to be similar than fraternal twins—identical twins share even more exact-match DNA.

- Maleness and femaleness, which are genetically programmed into us in the sense that XX and XY chromosomal pairs form our sex, are further ensconced in the genetic coding that wires the brains of boys and girls; this makes much of the behavior of males and females genetically marked behavior rather than behavior that is mainly socialized onto a blank slate.

- At this point, genetic researchers have been able to adroitly manipulate cells throughout the body, but they have not done as well with brain cells. There is a "blood-brain" barrier—that is, many cells of the brain remain more complicated than our science is presently able to appreciate. There is still—and always will be—some mystery left!

These, then, are a few of the secrets about our genetics that we are learning. As scientists pay attention to each, they find themselves face-to-face with ethical questions like: Should we clone humans? Final resolution of these ethical questions is generally not thought the province of parents and other community members. Scientists (and politicians) tend to like to answer these questions for all of us. Yet we all might weigh in, based on what we know at this point about the soul of the child. We might ask: Can cloning reproduce the light exactly, cell to cell, neuron to neuron? If it can't, then our attempt at creation is flawed. At this point, cloning cannot, especially given the blood-brain barrier. No laser is accurate enough to manipulate and fuse *all aspects of every cell*. Thus, at this point, all individual soul markings cannot be carried forward to the clone, especially subtle ones that control personality. Cloning still remains a flawed process. Will the blood-brain barrier one day be broken? If so, cloning may be able to exactly re-create the individual light, the soul markings, the divine child. If that day comes, we will face new questions.

Scientists ponder the question of cloning as they ponder all the ramifications of genetics and genome mapping. Their work will help some of us, over the next decades, who need medical help that only stem cell research can provide. Their work will probably, in our lifetimes, lead to the saving or the extension of a friend's or acquaintance's life. Their work may even lead to saving your own child's life. While in all statistical probability, most of us will not experience what Lindsey may well experience—a cure based on a parent's genetic research—all of us can benefit from the work done by Jim and so many others, for their work challenges each parent, each caregiver of children, and indeed our whole civilization to look at the developmental journey of our own children in a new light.

DOES YOUR CHILD HAVE A DESTINY?

"You talk so much, you're gonna be a lawyer," said my great-grandmother when I was about ten years old. I did not become a lawyer, making her seem less than prophetic. And yet, had my present profession—public speaking—existed in her life experience she might very well have said, "You talk so much, you're gonna be a public speaker." And she'd have been right.

I talked a lot as a child; my brother spoke very little. His genetic profile did not include as much development in the left hemisphere of the brain as mine, nor as much cross-talk between hemispheres. Mine included these things, giving me more speech fluency. My grandmother saw markings in me she couldn't quite explain, except in a cryptic phrase, but she did clearly see them.

Among the Shavante tribe in Brazil, profiled in anthropologist David Maybury-Lewis's *Millennium* television series, a man named Paolo was told by his grandfather when he was a little boy that he would "walk among the whites (Caucasians)," and teach them of the Shavante. At twenty-eight years old, Paolo became the subject of a television series created by a few Caucasians and shown to millions of others.

In Japan, a young girl, Mitsua, was told by her grandmother that she would become a great Kabuki actress. At eighteen, she became this actress, and continued on the stage into her fifties.

In each of these cases, someone close to a child read markings of that child's future in the soul of the child.

Geneticists tell us that by 2010 (optimistically), DNA tests on our children will be able to provide us with a detailed vision of the map our child is born with. DNA tests will reveal our children's predilections and tendencies, weaknesses and strengths, even down to how they will tolerate cigarettes, or whether they'll be shy. "By 2050," says Francis Collins of the National Human Genome Research Institute, "many potential diseases will be cured at the molecular level before they arise." At this point, however, geneticists have not found the genes for "lawyer," "teacher of the Caucasians," or "Kabuki actress." But let's ask ourselves: Even if geneticists haven't found them yet, can't they be revealed intuitively to those people—parents, grandparents, and other caregivers of children—most closely attached to the light of the child?

They already are. Every one of us, when we slow down to fully notice our child, notices certain inborn predilections and tendencies.

"He came out of the womb laughing," said the mother of Jerry Seinfeld in an interview on television.

"From very early, Steven was a moviemaker," said the mother of Steven Spielberg.

Gwyneth Paltrow's father told reporters she put on little plays for family audiences when just a toddler.

Christopher Columbus's mother reputedly could not keep her son, the young explorer, in her sights—he was always wandering down village streets, unafraid.

The science and the passion of genetics show us that each of us can glimpse the divine map our own child is born with. And it's not a single-destination map. Being a lawyer or teacher or actress is not all the map is about. It reveals many things to us, at different times. We say, "Jeremy is just like me when I was five." Or: "Mariah has a lot of her grandmother in her." We say, "No one's gonna hold Brittany back." Or: "Corbin is more sensitive than most boys." More than we realize, we intuit the divine map each child is born with, and we express and feel these intuitions in conversations with others we trust, in the hope that we can get a good grasp of that map so that we can guide our child's destiny. We do not see destiny as written in stone—but neither do we intuit that our child is simply an element of chaos in the world. We sense an inherent order in our child. We want to help reveal that order to the child and, through the child's life, to the world.

Once when I told my own story, a mom responded by saying, "I wouldn't say to a child what your great-grandmother said to you. I don't ever want to impose anything on my child. Let him just grow up." In a case like this, many people, with the best of intentions, turn away from their intuitions about the map or inherent order in the child. This parent hopes that by not ever intervening, not guiding, not being "an imposing parent," the child will discover a complete, independent individuality. This pure independence is thought to be of profound benefit, especially in our very individualistic society, in which the personal acquisition of success and independence is considered the ultimate destiny of all children.

Genetic and neurobiological research have shown some pitfalls in these views. First, the new sciences show us that our son becoming a lawyer or our daughter an engineer because of an imposing comment early in life is not generally possible. Even years of taking math, calculus, chemistry, or physics will not make someone an engineer who doesn't, by nature, have the right hemisphere brain development for highly spatial tasks. In cases where the child can be influenced into a career by parents, grandparents, or others, the influencer would have to *constantly pressure* and mold the child. For instance, a father would have to force a son into his business by constant pressure; a mother (and a society) would have to pressure a daughter, by withholding opportunity, to give up her dreams of being a lawyer or engineer. These things do happen.

In most present postindustrial societies, however, they are now the exceptions. Most children (unfortunately, not all, especially those living in poverty) advance through life with opportunity before them, and parents work hard so that their children can take opportunities. Most children do not become lawyers or teachers or actresses because of one simple statement made by a wise person in a child's life. In my case, Paolo's, and Mitsua's, one statement did not form the child into the public speaker, tribal teacher, or actress. DNA research has shown us that the child is born with abilities and inclinations toward these destinies. The role of the grandparent was not to mold the child to a certain destiny; rather, the grandparent was able to *see into the soul of the child, and report what he or she saw.*

Each child is born with a DNA combination unique to the child (what we've called, in the context of religious language, "a divine map"). For caregiving adults *not* to vocalize their intuitive revelations of that map, for us *not* to gently guide the child along the course of those revelations—this would be the less beneficial course. To pretend that one has *not* seen a bit of the destiny of a child is to withhold from that child the very love and attachment that the searching child yearns for. A child does not want to wander aimlessly during twenty years of crucial development. To be told he or she has no destiny, just "opportunity," may also—especially if the child senses a life course within but can't quite grasp it—do the child a disservice. Though I did not become a lawyer, I directed my life energy in high school toward speech and debate, having listened to the wisdom of my own soul as voiced by my grandmother (and my mother and father, who seconded her intuition), and those years of learning to speak in public have allowed me to be a fluent, self-confident speaker and teacher. Had no one ever said to me "You should be a lawyer," the dominoes might not have fallen effectively in place the way they have for me to be happily fulfilled by my life of public service.

In every child is the inborn urge to belong; the wise parent and caregiver is the one who looks into the light of the child's behavior and takes the risk of saying, "Here your destiny might be. Come, look at this. Is this you? Why not give it a try?" Because destiny is not a single thing but many paths in one path, the wise one may well find many occasions to say the same words.

Will geneticists and the new sciences ever be able to actually lay out a child's destiny for us? Will it be like reading tea leaves or a crystal ball? "I see by your son's DNA that he will be a lawyer and raise two children." "I see by your daughter's DNA that she will be an engineer and raise three children."

This kind of scenario, subject perhaps of a science fiction novel a hundred years ago, is actually half-conceivable now. But only half-conceivable. DNA cannot take into account randomness—for example, how many children we will have—or other circumstantial influences—such as the effect on us of where we live and how we are raised. Scientists cannot, ultimately, substitute for parents and other loved ones. Science guides and encourages but does not love and raise the child. We, our children, and their mentors will best intuit a child's destiny.

We parents and other caregivers know best how to read the light that is our child. In life's small things we can notice our child's attempts at divine focus and destiny:

- We see how desperately our children want to discover an activity (and activities) in which to immerse themselves and their light.

- We observe them seeking a purpose—helping Mom cook, taking out the garbage. We often joke that our kids don't want to do their chores, and often they don't; but just as often, they will bound into the kitchen ready to help, to be a part of things.

- We notice that they show their desperation for our help with questions of destiny (even when they resist us), questions like "Who am I?" "Where did I come from?" "Is there a plan?"

- We notice that they seek the stimulation not only of activity but also of silence, often pulling away into solitude in order to listen to themselves, then returning to us with questions and answers.

- We watch as they yearn to be the primary authors of their own destiny, especially as they sense that greater forces—God or Nature—are more powerful than they. We notice that they yearn to be heroes and heroines of a destiny provided by the greater forces, whether in their religious life, or a movie, or a video game.

- From very early on, we sense that each of our children carries individual burdens. Often we will find ourselves watching our child who, like the Greek figure Sisyphus, seems to be pushing a boulder up a hill, with the boulder rolling back down, the child pushing it up again, over and over; and we will remember doing this ourselves, and we will say, "It's going to be all right. You're learning a part of who you are from this burden." And in this we will be guiding destiny.

- We may well stand at our child's wedding and say, "Here stand two souls, designed by God to come together." Our child may, years later, go through a divorce with this person whom we all thought a soul mate—yet this does not disfigure the initial idea that, even if for but a time, our child and this soul mate were designed to come together.

- Watching our children grow, we may need to constantly alter our sense of what destiny is. We may have started with the idea that our child would be a CEO or a football player, then realize our son's ultimate destiny was to work in a less glamorous job and raise children, our daughter's to be a mother, a leader, or mentor, or a combination of many things.

- We may well hear the call of *mission* in our children, from our children, or from an elder. Laurie Beth Jones, in her book, *The Path*, writes of her father who told her that in World War II, an unidentified soldier walking toward a group would be automatically shot if he couldn't state his *mission*. In this context, Jones wonders what our world would be like if being able to know and articulate our *mission* was a life and death necessity every day. It would, in her words, "force millions of us to reexamine who we are . . . and save immeasurable amounts of money, tears and heartache. . . . Those who have never known what it is like to feel passionate commitment to a cause would be catapulted from their couches onto the playing field . . . and in the process come fully alive." What a different life the undestined child would have if we applied ourselves to helping him or her be the child who can know and articulate a life mission.

It may be our urge, especially when our children are young, to build self-confidence by saying, "You are pretty (handsome), intelligent, athletic, and a good person," cataloging traits we want to build in the child; this general approach will rarely hurt, but it may also give way, at some point, to more specific praise for specific actions: "You sure write well." "You sure do care about people." Specific praise builds in the child a sense of mission, and the ability to pursue a purposeful self. When praised for those elements of mission and destiny that are specific, the adolescent child experiences clearer soul growth.

Throughout our time with our children, we will find them seeking their "calling," and we will make mistakes in our guidance of their search. We will point them in one direction, and they will resist, moving in another. There will be fighting between us. Even in this, though, our child will find our help beneficial as he or she seeks a destiny. In destiny is the inherent, safe order the child inherently seeks—the safe order already marked and hidden within. When that inherent order is felt, the child's core self is safe, and the child's authentic power limitless.

Attachment and Destiny

In order to fully understand divine markings in our child, we spend time with the child—attached—*completing the child* by our presence. Our intuition of the soul's destiny is only as clear as our intimacy and closeness with the child.

During my family therapy practice, I often noticed parents and children carrying on what I called "long-distance relationships." This metaphor is based on a kind of romantic relationship, in which one lover lives, for months, in a city far away from the other. Statistically, these long-distance romances have a very high failure rate. The lovers are unable to remain attached and bonded to each other because they do not spend enough time together.

What we've learned about the human soul provides us a neuro-physical explanation for the statistical difficulty with these long-distance relationships. The cells of one soul do not spend enough time with the cells of another to remain bonded, light to light, person to person, soul to soul.

In the same way, many parents now raise children in long-distance relationships. Often they live in the same home (though often not, because of divorce), yet they spend little time together, little time understanding and loving each other. Both parents and children are economic interns, whose most important job is social and financial success, whether in the present—in the case of the parents who measure themselves mainly by workplace prowess—or in the future—in the case of the kids, who must rush from activity to school to TV or Internet entertainment in search of society's formulas for belonging.

In these long-distance relationships, it is nearly impossible for the parent (much less grandparent or other extended family member) to read the destiny of the child, to see the treasure marked on the soul of the child. As in all things involving the light in and around the human body, attachment and love are the great reflectors of light. The light reveals itself best to those who love unconditionally, with formidable presence, and with their eyes open to the divine destiny that the child is trying to hold forth.

In my family practice, I discovered that sometimes the parents who pushed their children into a myriad of activities during a given week were parents who practiced inadequate attachment with their children, especially with their adolescents. These parents had infinitely high expectations for the child that were based less on the child's soul markings and more on the parents'. Every parent—including myself—is prone to throw children into activities, or push them toward activities we enjoyed (or missed) as children; push them toward peers and communities external to the family in hopes of "providing them all the opportunities possible." We do this without realizing that the child who is fully and happily attached to parents and loved ones (even during adolescent resistance) is most likely to grow the self-confidence to make it in the world, and to find his or her personal destiny. The child needs the attachment first, the myriad activities second.

"But I don't believe in destiny," a parent might say. "Nothing is prewritten. We're in complete control of our lives." If one believes in God (and most people in the world know there is a unifying force in the universe) to say that nothing is prewritten is simply a form of arrogance that is countered inwardly by one's own belief in God. And even if one does not believe in God but only in science, the new sciences have shown, in these chapters, how divinely prewritten much of human life already is. The new sciences have shown us God.

Having said these things about soul markings and about destiny, we have certainly left one soul marking out: evil. Is evil marked onto the genome? Let us not turn away from dealing with that very difficult soul marking. Was Hitler destined to become Hitler? When a mother sits in a courtroom and watches her son, Ted Bundy, sentenced to death, can we not help but wonder, Couldn't she have done more? and Why did he turn out that way?

WHAT IS EVIL?

I have worked with individuals I considered to be evil (let us define *evil* as a complete lack of compassion for other life-forms), but only one who utterly frightened me. A man in his forties serving three consecutive life sentences, he appeared in my life during the years I was a contract counselor at a prison.

What markings existed on his soul?

He had been beaten and sexually abused as a boy; this played a large part in his later behavior—he was a rapist and a murderer. But many people are beaten and sexually abused, and they do not appear before us with cold, lifeless eyes, and a complete lack of compassion. Generous frontal lobe activity (empathy and morality in the brain) remains for them, and they raise families and live compassionate lives. Why does one victim become evil while another does not?

Part of the answer lies in the marks on the soul. The science of genetics has recently taught us the biological roots of evil. Genetic studies, studies of adoptive children, and studies of twins have all shown a genetic proclivity (not an absolute assurance) toward the kinds of brain and thought disorders that lead to evil behavior.

Studies of children born to biological parents with antisocial personality disorders show that those children have a greater tendency toward developing those disorders, *even if a child is nurtured by parents without the disorders.*

Studies of children with schizophrenia or other potentially socially destructive thought disorders show a genetic proclivity in the parental lineage toward the disorder.

Studies of twins whose parents are antisocial show that these twins have an equal proclivity toward antisocial behavior, whether they are raised by their biological parents or not.

In summary, the term used to describe the trait detected in these kinds of studies is "heritability." The "sins of the parents," as it were, are inherited by the child—they are marked on the child's DNA.

This is one way of acknowledging the soul marking we call evil. Another way is to PET scan the human brain and notice evil in that light.

The psychiatrist Daniel Amen, who is one of the best at employing PET and SPECT scans to study brain anomalies, recently completed a study of fifty murderers and two hundred other violent felons. "Without exception," he discovered, "all show reduced activity in the prefrontal cortex [seat of judgment, planning and thoughtfulness], overactivity in the anterior cingulate gyrus [the brain's gearshift, which allows it to segue from one thought to another] and abnormalities in the left temporal lobe [involved in mood and temper control]." Amen explains: "If you have a left-temporal-lobe problem, you have dark, awful, violent thoughts. If you have a cingulate-gyrus problem as well, you get stuck on bad thoughts. And if you have a prefrontal-cortex problem, you can't supervise the bad thoughts you get stuck on."

In this simple way, Amen shows us some of the markings on the soul using technology that scans the light of the brain.

Other physical tests show us other marks of antisociality and evil in the soul. Skin conductance activity—speed of electromagnetic conductance on the skin—is lower among criminals than non-criminals. Lower resting heart rate levels (HRLs) show up in criminals, and can be used as predictors of criminal behavior. Pulse rates were examined in 1,813 male eleven-year-old children. Among this group, those who had been in trouble with the police had lower HRLs than the other schoolchildren.

Electrodermal, cardiovascular, and cortical tests all show differences between the light, the soul, of those children prone to criminal, antisocial, and evil behavior, and those not. Quite literally, the light of the antisocial or potentially evil child is different from the light of the more compassionate child.

These, then, are different ways in which the new sciences can help us trace the marks of "bad behavior" and of, in some cases, evil on the human soul (though we would not want to think that they necessarily always indicate evil—for instance, many people who have low pulse rates are not evil); but even then, these markings are not the whole picture of why a person becomes evil. Among those individuals we know as evil—from Hitler to Jeffrey Dahmer—those individuals whose eyes may be cold, whose behavior is not compassionate, whose individual actions or whose social leadership are defined by their attempts to destroy others, evil is obviously marked on the soul, but it is covertly and historically aggravated by one or more of the predominant forms of *violence* in family and social systems. In the family (and neighborhood, school, faith community, and extended family), these forms of violence would be: abuse, neglect, sexual molestation, emotional incest, excessive shaming and manipulation, breakdown of family attachment, or other chronic life-altering stress. In the larger society, some form of poverty, social shame, or racial abuse can add to the violence or neglect practiced in the family.

Soul markings are genetic, but the brain also gets rewired by violence, which then becomes a new soul marking, left by this lifetime's experience on the child.

Quite simply, when a child experiences constant abuse or neglect, he or she has a greater chance of turning out evil. When they are raised in trauma, males, by a genetic proclivity I've explored in *A Fine Young Man,* have a greater statistical probability of taking on overtly violent forms of evil than do females. All children raised by divorced parents or single parents show a statistically higher incidence of crime, for instance, with males constituting 90 percent of these instances. Females, by a genetic proclivity I've explored in *The Wonder of Girls,* are more likely, when raised in violence or other constant stresses, to develop eating disorders or clinical depression (which can lead, at times, to violence).

Violence and lack of emotional safety raise cortisol (stress hormone) levels in the child, blunting brain growth—which causes a lack of growth in prefrontal and temporal lobes, and overactivity in the cingulate gyrus. These raised cortisol levels ultimately affect our pulse, heart rate, even cellular activity in our skin. The trauma to all our cells created by an increase in stress hormones throughout our cellular system kills off needed brain and other cells; and it skews the growth of many others. Also, many cells simply die, for they do not get used—cells in the prefrontal cortex, the temporal lobe, the skin. Some of the human flame, the soul of the child, is extinguished. That flame grows when a child is hugged and cared for. The flame grows less generously when the child is mistreated by the caregiver or simply not embraced enough. Children growing up in insecure attachment, without enough holding by caregivers, show higher cortisol levels, less regulation of brain-body activity, and decreased electromagnetic activity in the whole brain.

This fact, established now by new technologies, is especially frightening in an era in which, during the most vulnerable childhood years, birth to three, less and less physical contact is going on between caregivers and children, and in the second most vulnerable age, puberty and early adolescence, less social contact is going on between parents and children. This has a direct bearing on how soul markings for bad behavior and for evil evidence themselves in later life.

Where our ancestral mothers and grandmothers carried their infants on their backs while they went to work in the fields or the market, today we mothers, fathers, and other caregivers are not able to carry our infants around with us when we work (we work away from our babies), thus cutting the infant off from soul-to-soul contact during a very vulnerable time.

When I was asked to study reports of all of the boys who committed murder in schools—from Jonesboro, Arkansas, to Littleton, Colorado—I was not surprised to discover that all of them had experienced one or more of the crucial elements for antisocial and evil behavior: lack of attachment at crucial times (especially during infancy and puberty), some form of abuse or violence, broken caregiving systems, and/or developmental epochs of general neglect. I named their condition Character Regression Syndrome: inadequate attachment during a pivotal developmental epoch, which impeded frontal and temporal lobe growth; combined with family trauma or violence, which affected cingulate gyrus/limbic functioning; in turn influenced by an adolescent trigger—for instance, the experience of being bullied. This combination of elements led to regression of the boy's character (moral action) to the level of a young child who does not fully understand consequences and outcomes. "Man's character is his fate," said the Greek philosopher Heraclitus. For these school shooters, this was indeed true.

In all this—from the obvious and overt beating and sexual abuse of children, to coldness toward the child, to lack of family contact at crucial times, in conjunction with our understanding of genetics—we can now better understand what evil is (in a biological sense) and where it comes from. We can understand why one child, brought up in difficult circumstances, turns out relatively well, and another turns out so angry at the world, so indifferent, so hateful, and so dangerous. When we say "He's a good soul" or "She's a good soul," we mean two things compounded together: We mean that his or her soul was marked with greater or lesser potential for evil, *and* that those who loved that soul helped embellish the good and made sure to overlay the potential "bad" with human love and compassion. We can put it this way: We are born both in original sin and original blessing. Our souls are marked for good and bad. The question each of us must answer is simple: How will I nurture the soul of the child so thoroughly that whatever dark markings exist can be assuaged, within the soul of the child, by the light?

We know far more, now, because of PET and SPECT scans, EEGs, and skin conductivity tests about the exact methods by which the original blessing can be submerged and the original sin accentuated in the growing child. Over the next few decades, as this research becomes public, each parent will realize how much the future of civilization depends as much on individual parents as it does on armies.

Violence and the Peace Rock

The author Astrid Lindgren has written a beautiful essay called "Peace Rock." It tells a story reflective of what we're discussing.

"When I was about twenty years old, I met a pastor's wife who told me that when she was young and had her first child, she didn't believe in striking children, although spanking kids with a switch pulled from a tree was standard punishment at the time. One day when her son was four or five, he did something she felt warranted a spanking—the first of his life. She told him to go outside and find a switch for her. The boy was gone a long time. When he came back, he was crying. He said to her, 'Mama, I couldn't find a switch, but here's a rock you can throw at me.'

"Suddenly the mother understood the situation from the child's point of view: 'If my mother wants to hurt me, then it makes no difference what she does it with. She might as well do it with a stone.' The mother took the boy onto her lap and they both cried. She laid the rock on a shelf in the kitchen to remind herself forever—never violence."

Lindgren concludes:

"That is something everyone should keep in mind—because violence begins in the nursery."

Lindgren knows, of course, that this event could have taken place with a father, or with another person, and the incident with the rock is symbolic of a million possible incidents of violence and broken safety nets.

There are many kinds of violence—the withholding of love is one kind; hitting another; emotional manipulation another. Each does violence to the soul of the child. Each can lead the child toward evil. A single swat on the bottom now and then, as part of a larger, compassionate discipline system, may actually help a soul grow, just like a little guilt now and then can be a good thing. These may not be violence—they may be part of good attachment and a family's worthy discipline system. Beautifully attached to her child, the mother, in the peace rock story, understood that she had nearly practiced not good attachment and discipline, but violence, and the boy learned far more from her tears, and his own, than if she had doggedly continued her initial course. This mother knew that soul flourishes where love is sewn. It is deleted where love is not. Gradations of soul growth occur in direct relationship to gradations of love received. Each child is marked for greater or lesser resiliency to the lack of love received, but all children are marked with the need for love. Each adult is challenged, when caring for a child, as well as when caring for any vulnerable life, to find ourselves in the gradations of giving.

Our religious teachers have pointed us, very visually, using light, in this direction. Think for a moment of Jesus and Mary, so often depicted in paintings and stained-glass windows as figures bathed in light. Are not the paintings scientifically accurate—would not Jesus and Mary, in the *Pietà*, have tested on PETs, SPECTS, and skin conductivity as very "lit up?"

Satan, Lucifer, or the "devil" is so often depicted in religious texts as being just the opposite. Satan lives in darkness. If there were a Satan we could hook up to monitors, we would discover that he (or she, to be fair) would emit less light and—by experiencing inwardly that greater darkness—would wish greater darkness on others. Evil in the soul begets evil in the world.

Evil then—along with the disorders that it gives rise to, the narcissism, the paranoia, the antisocial personality disorders—is marked on the soul, but human society and individual families have the ability to choose how to handle the marking. This is the ultimate truth the new sciences teach us about soul markings. Our children are born with a divine map, but we are the keepers, the soul tenders, who guide the child to discover the full scope of that divinity. When the child enters the darkness and never returns, we have shared responsibility for our neglect of the light. Parents and other caregivers do not create evil in the child—it is created before we receive the child into our lives. Yet it is also fair to say that we are the creators of the evil in our child. Both are true. Polylogical thinking about evil is needed and can reap rewards.

Taking this kind of responsibility does not answer, however, the larger question: Why is the soul of one child marked with greater evil than another, and why, ultimately, is any soul marked for evil at all? The new sciences do not yet have answers to these questions; we only know that the soul is so marked, and that evil began with genetically marked souls.

We also know that death is inevitable even if we don't know why. Let's look at death now. The new sciences do not tell us why the soul of the child, and of the adult, is marked for dying and for death, but they have recently taught us a great deal about death that sheds new light on our wonderings. This new information pertains greatly to the divine map each of us is born with.

WHAT IS DEATH?

Our children are divine, the eternal flame of the universe. They existed before birth and yet could not exist until birth; they will both exist and not exist after death, their soul markings continuing on in their progeny. Neuroscience and genetics remove any doubt we may have had about our children's (and our own) infinitude. "If there is a God," my friend Jim said, "it must be in the genome." There are numerous ways in which we are the eternal flame, not the least of which is the existence of DNA.

And yet we do not feel the grace of infinitude when our child dies. We feel absolute despair. It feels like our child is gone forever.

What is death? Has our child really died?

The former Catholic priest, now author and philosopher, James A. Connor writes of life in beautiful terms.

"Existence is a flame," he says. "What is the universe but a twelve-billion-year-old flame? What is a tree but slow burning fire? What is an animal (or human) but a fire that burns faster? The Spirit is likened to flame, either to flame or to wind, the feeder of flame. Even when I am not filled with the Holy Spirit, my body is a fire, oxidizing on the spot, a heat engine balanced on the blade of too much heat or too little, held in check by the structures of my cells."

In Chapters 1 and 2, we came to realize that we are, as humans, an oxidizing fire, balancing hot and cold in our cell structure. We traced how our children flower in flames of self-discovery, individualization, and self-realization. In this chapter, we have noted the hidden markings on the flame, markings we must look for carefully if we are to see them through the smoke and incandescence of children's lives and cultures. We ourselves have each lived the life of heat and light, and we have guarded our children against that which we fear most: the death of our son or daughter, the end of existence, the flame going out.

The writer D. H. Lawrence, as he was dying, described his vision of the living soul. "Out of eternity a thread separates itself on the blackness, a horizontal thread that fumes a little upon the dark." Lawrence cautioned us to notice the inherent fragility and vulnerability of this thread of light. The very sun itself, he wrote, that seemingly endless bounty of flame, "is pivoted upon the core of pure oblivion, so is a candle, even a match." The flaming soul is vulnerable; it can easily blow out. Lawrence's word for what is left when the thread is gone is a fine, old word we all, at some visceral level, fear: *oblivion*. We fear it especially when it is our own child who faces oblivion, or our own imaginations that face, on a daily basis, fears that we have not done enough to keep that child safe.

Do the neurosciences teach us new things about death? Can we see beyond the flame, then the extinguishment of that flame, the fear of oblivion, then the absorption of the soul—and all its beautiful markings—into oblivion? We can. Yes. We now have a better understanding of death and the way that soul markings might pass from life to life.

The Light of Death

For the organism we call "the body" to live, there must be a minimum of electrical activity—of heat and flame—in the structure of its cells. Just as everyone has a unique fingerprint, each body has its own unique threshold for that minimum, based on each person's metabolism, heart rate, and brain wave patterns. This threshold-minimum of electrical activity in the cells must be maintained for life (breathing) to continue.

We can see this concept operating in people who have a physical disability—for instance, paralysis of a limb. There is little electrical activity in the cells in that limb. Muscles atrophy from lack of electrical activity. In a sense, they don't breathe. In the same way, the human neurocardio-pulmonary system (brain/heart/lungs) must maintain a minimum of electrical activity—of light. This minimum in turn maintains activity in cells throughout the body. Death is, in this context, a severe shock to the neurocardio-pulmonary system—a severe shock to the electric pulsing in the field of matter we call "the body." Cell activity weakens, then ends. The body desists its speed-of-light interactions long enough for matter to go nearly completely dark.

We say "nearly completely" because a tiny residue of light activity does continue past the minimum activity threshold. When a person dies, for instance, hair keeps growing on the body, though at a very decelerated rate. It can take many days before that hair stops growing. Why does the hair keep growing? There is electromagnetic activity, though it is highly dissipated (what is called "residual activity"). Similarly, after clinical death, people have "thoughts and visions." In separate studies conducted around the world by such researchers as Elisabeth Kübler-Ross, Harold Moody, and Moody's disciple Dannion Brinkley, people in all cultures report similar "after death" experiences. In each, there is a vision of white light (some call these angels); there is a dark tunnel; there are generally groups of people who appear to be of our ancestry and soul marking; and there is what Brinkley has called "life review"—in the visionary state, the dying person reviews his or her life.

Neuroscientists have brought to the study of these worldwide reports their brain-scan technology. They now understand that the brain still experiences electromagnetic pulsing for a brief time, even after the brain-heart-lungs continuum is below the minimum required activity. They can track where activity is by two methods: by scanning the brains of people who are just dying, and by comparing the reports of people who have returned from clinical death with what we already know of the brain. In both cases, we notice residual activity in the parietal lobe, which houses our brain's orientation areas; the temporal lobe, which houses a great deal of our religious feeling (some have simplistically called this "the God part of the brain"); the frontal lobe, which houses moral thinking; and the hippocampus, which houses a great deal of memory. It comes as little surprise that people who have died (then returned to tell about it) report remembering ancestors (residual hippocampal activity), moving out of this world into another world (parietal disorientation activity), having visions and religious experiences (temporal activity), and making moral judgments on themselves (frontal lobe activity).

When a child is killed by a drunk driver, the neurocardio-pulmonary alliance by which cell activity maintains the necessary minimum of electrical momentum is traumatized, and the structure of all the cells is altered. When hospital monitors that are hooked up to a preemie baby, or a newborn, or any sick person show the end of electrical activity, we call it flatlining. Pulse rate no longer bounces up and down in green thready light but now becomes a green flat line. In order to try to remotivate the neurocardio-pulmonary alliance, electric shock is applied to the heart. "Clear!" the EMT worker cries out. "Clear!" Hopefully electric shock can reshock the system into working.

If that does not work (and, in the case of the sick, when other methods are exhausted), the person is deemed dead. The light goes out of the sick child's eyes. The minimum-required electricity goes out of her skin, which becomes very pale. The light goes out of his brain, as a PET scans shows so little light left inside there, then a few hours later, none at all. Our child, so young, has entered oblivion, and we weep in grief and pain.

Yet there is something immortal that has happened in the life process our child engaged in, for however long that engagement lasted. It has directly to do with soul markings, and we can notice it now, in our thinking. I suspect, in a few hundred years, we will have the neural technology (or the direct neural ability) to see it "empirically." We only now use about 12 percent of our brain capacity—at some point in our history, we'll use 20 or 30 percent, and at that time we'll be able to know things, see things, and sense things (by using personal experiences and technological research) that now we can only surmise.

One thing we'll empirically show is immortality: That the soul of the child (Augustine's "soul that is the light of the body," the Buddhist "lamp," the Jewish "sliver of light," the Zoroastrian "flame") is not some abstract idea called psyche or soul that inhabits a body for five, ten, or ninety years and then leaves the body untouched by experience, but, in fact, that the soul has been *marked* by its life as a cell structure; light has been marked by its journey through the prism of human experience, and those markings will never die. Perhaps we'll gain the brain power to prove empirically what psychics (not the con artists, but real psychics, like John Edward) see as they tell you everything you know (and even what you don't know) about your great-grandmother who is trying to talk to you from the world of the dead, or can recall for you a secret incident that occurred between yourself and your now-dead child. Brain-scan equipment should show us that these psychics are using more than 12 percent of the brain; in doing so, they are "reading the markings" left on your memory and, presumably, the residual soul of your dead great-grandmother or dead child.

If you have had an experience with a real psychic that "blew your mind"—I, a researcher in neuroscience, remain skeptical as long as I can until I am faced, as I have been more than once, with psychics who not only read my mind, but also seemed to read the minds of the dead—you may wonder how to make sense of the experience. "How could he know that?" you say, turning to someone close to you. Or: "This sounds like Grandma is talking to me right now."

No matter what your level of skepticism, it is worth wondering about this particular idea:

Is it possible that when we die, the light we are, which we already know remains for a time in the brain and even in hair follicles, actually remains nearby (whether like air near us or in some other dimensional space and time our brains have not yet understood)? Our optical nerves, and our senses, are very limited—we use only a little of our brains. We may not be able to see the light of a soul that is not embodied and therefore living-in-matter. Light is an infinite spectrum; there are many kinds of light our eyes simply cannot see. When people see "ghosts" or "angels," isn't it possible they are seeing different kinds of light, nonordinary light by our optical standards? Is it possible that in a thousand years we may actually have instruments or have developed the brain's ability to see these spectrums? This may completely change our understanding of death as "dark oblivion."

Until that time, we have some "proof"—loosely defined—that not only does the light we are continue after the neurocardio-pulmonary shock we call death, but also that the light has been changed, altered, modified by life experience. Proof for both—

again, loosely defined—comes to us in personal experiences. I have had an experience of meeting a loved one who died. This experience involved no intercession of a psychic. My best friend, during my late teens, Mike Garvey, died at eighteen while hiking; he appeared to me, a few days later, while I was driving my 1966 Chevy Nova. There is no doubt in my mind as to what happened—I saw a light, then a projected figure of my friend, and he spoke to me quite extensively, telling me things I had not known about him when he lived. For now, given the technologies we have, this personal proof is all that I have of the continuation of light beyond the cells of the body.

The physicist Fred Alan Wolf lost his son. A neighbor, drunk and stoned, crashed his car into Wolf's house, killing son Michael in his bed. As Wolf expressed, in his book on physics *The Eagle's Quest,* "nothing can describe the horror and pain of the loss of one's child." But as he further expressed, Michael did not completely die. Michael appeared to him a number of times. "Over the past few years," he writes, "I have felt Michael's presence." In a dream, he spoke to his son, whose ashes he had just flung over ocean waters. In Wolf's mind, as in mine—and, if polls are correct, in the minds of millions of people—the light of the dead does not fully go out at the second of death. Is this proof that light continues after the body dies? It is a kind of proof.

Proof like this is also all we have thus far to show us that the "person" who comes to us as light, or as words transmitted through a psychic, is not an unchanged soul. This person has been marked and formed by existence, and speaks to us from the lexicon of existence. The "Michael" who comes to Fred Alan Wolf is the Michael who had lived under his roof, grown, changed, become marked—not some pristine Michael who had never been born into this life. My best friend, Mike Garvey, also appeared in my car as he was, at eighteen, after years of following his soul markings and divine map through eighteen years of soul growth.

No wonder the Hindus (and other Asians) believe in reincarnation—the constant rebirth of souls into new material bodies (whether human, animal, or plant). If we say reincarnation is the idea that souls constantly inhabit new material forms when they can no longer inhabit a previous material form, we would more closely approximate what the new sciences, when they ponder these "religious things," might say polylogically: Electromagnetic energy cannot be destroyed. Even at physical death, energy continues in some form and may have the capability—though we can't yet prove this empirically—to inhabit, serially, more than one material form (more than one body). Furthermore, karma (the idea that your newest incarnation is marked with what you learned in your last) might make real sense. The soul is changed by life, and the light of the soul marked from previous lives is then newly marked in this life.

For many people, there is not yet enough empirical proof to convince them that death, while a painfully real wrenching of ourselves from those we love, is also an illusion.

"There is no death," say the Buddhists.

As the use of neurotechnologies continues to progress over the years, we should not be surprised to learn that death is an illusion, that it is not oblivion, that we are immortal, and thus: that we are God. This challenging realization will not mean what many people mean when they say "immortal." It is a frightening idea for most of us, who consider the idea "I am God" to be heresy. But, in fact, if the light is immortal and we are the light, then we must rethink our sense of ourselves and of the God we've known. Amazing things can happen for each of us, for humanity, and for our children, when we realize that God is not above us, beyond us, angry at us, or a single prophet; God is not separate from us in any way. Death and separation between ourselves and God only exist in our thinking, and our thinking can mature beyond these ideas.

Amazing things happen when we fully realize that *we are God*. Fully realizing this is a precursor to fully realizing that our children are God. And fully realizing that will change our view of children. Fully realizing the divine nature of the child requires us to constantly push toward the edges of new thinking. In the next three chapters, the sciences of neurophysics, neuropsychology, and sociobiology will help us go even further than the discoveries we've made in these first three chapters—that we can prove the existence of the soul, help it grow, and discover the divine map of its growth. These new sciences will now help us discover what we may have known intuitively all along: In our most beautiful moments of union with our children, God is our child.

PART II

God Is the Child

The aim of each thing we do is to make the lives of
our children richer and more possible.

— AUDRE LORDE

4

THE NEW HUMAN: HOW OUR THINKING MUST CHANGE

The future of the human being lies in the free invention of the human mind.

—Albert Einstein

Albert Einstein is one of the heroes of modern civilization. He understood light. He laid the groundwork not only for the greatest and most frightening use of light imaginable—the nuclear bomb—but also the PET and SPECT scans, lasers, and infrared technologies we've referred to in Part I. While various men and women throughout history have directly altered the way we feel about life, very few have affected our everyday lives, and the possibilities for the raising of our children, like Einstein. He changed how we feel and what we do by helping us to change the way we think.

If we take the time to fully contemplate his ideas, it is possible to get the feeling of being a student in the eternal academy. We each become able to search for the doorways of our civilization; we gain an immense depth in the way we care for people around us. Albert Einstein taught us how to do these things with the intention of making simple and apprehensible what is complicated and intimidating about the universe; he promised, simultaneously, to retain the mystery of the infinitely mysterious, for there is nothing worse than human beings pretending they know more than they do.

For Einstein, the beauty of nature and the human ability to discover nature's truths was, first and foremost, a matter of *thinking*, not of laboratory experiments. Einstein believed in changing the world through *thought*—what he called *"the free invention of the human mind."* From that free invention, he argued, came understanding of nature's truths, which laboratory and mathematical experiments would then corroborate. His love of free thought was one of the ways in which Einstein differed from other scientists of his time. Another was his commitment to use science for the betterment of human and natural life. Perhaps his most profound regret was that it seemed, when he was dying, that his science of light, which led to the creation of the atomic bomb, might destroy the children of the world.

Born in Ulm, Germany, Albert Einstein began his life as a young boy interested in both science and religion. His father managed a small electro-chemical plant, while his mother managed the family's development. His father directed him more toward science, his mother toward religion. When Albert was five, his father gave him a pocket compass, which intrigued and moved him. The compass needle pointed in the same direction, no matter how he manipulated the compass itself! He would later tell friends that this moment as a child moved him to understand that "something deeply hidden had to be behind nature and human life."

Between 1902 and 1909, when he was a young man, he

worked in a Swiss Patent Office in Bern, Switzerland, where in his free time he began his thinking about light, and from there, about nature, human nature, and God. He developed some of his famous theories (for example, e = mc²; or, energy equals mass times the velocity of light squared) during this time. He posited that light could be thought of as a stream of tiny particles, or *quanta*. Once light was explained as particles, physics changed. To get a sense of how completely physics, then human life, changed after Einstein, consider not just PET scans, which most people never see, but also your television, or a computer, or today's movies. None would have been possible without the idea that light is quanta.

Einstein's suggestion that there is equivalence between energy and matter became a basis for the success of the Allies during World War II. Many thinkers have credited our civilization's victory of freedom over oppression to Einstein's ideas about the manipulation of energy, mass, and light. He himself felt beleaguered by this kind of applause; yet, it is hard to deny that without the atomic bomb, the war might have gone a different way.

Perhaps the most intriguing and least discussed of Einstein's contributions to your and to my life (and most germane to the leap in thinking and in loving that we seek to inspire in this book) is the hidden heart behind the idea that energy and mass are equivalent, and that light is quanta. The heartfelt idea behind these Einsteinian theories was his own deep religious feelings. Later in his life, especially after World War II, Einstein devoted himself to proving his unified field theory: that everything, everyone, all matter, all energy, are unified, are all one field. Einstein clearly believed this as a matter of faith—he was a deeply religious man—but could not prove it mathematically. He was dissatisfied with his general and special theories of relativity because no matter how elegant their thinking and their experimental corroboration, they could not include electromagnetism. He cautioned humanity not to be satisfied until a unified field theory was proven that did include electromagnetism.

By the end of Einstein's life his theory was not fully proven by the field of mathematics. To this day, we are unable to "do the math" that proves the unified field theory.

On the other hand: Is there only one way to do math?

UNIFYING THE FIELD

As we have made the journey of this book together, we have done so in the hope of arriving at one single and common goal: To find the deepest clues, the deepest inspiration, and the most important directions for our families, our civilization, and the care of our children. Albert Einstein, biological father of three children, stepfather of two, would hold our objective as the highest human goal. He hoped to prove the unified field theory in order to bring peace to humanity. He worried most for the children of a nuclear age, an age in which the manipulation of light could lead both to the truths of nature and to absolute danger.

In Part I of this book, we took a glance at light and saw how it refracts as the soul of the child. We employed the sciences of neurochemistry, neurobiology, and genetics in order to make our exploration. Einstein would certainly have us do more. Fettered by mathematical formulation, he could not even go as far as we have; but he wanted to go further. Toward the end of his life, he gave us all a clue as to how to make the leap in the thinking that he wanted to make. He was asked about his religion (born a Jew, he became a well-assimilated American who lived in Princeton, New Jersey, from his midthirties to his death); he said that he knew himself as a religious man of monotheistic Judaism, and yet he also felt that a human belief in a personal, monotheistic God was too specific—the Being that unites and is the creative force of the universe, he felt, was personal and could certainly be called "he" or "she"; yet, to Einstein, God was something else too.

Albert Einstein, in his particular genius, is a wonderful starting point for our exploration in this chapter of the new human, of religion, and of the kinds of parents and families we can become in the future. He is an excellent starting point not only because he made possible our understanding of soul as light, but also because he posited a science of God, a neurophysics, which we can utilize in ways he might admire.

Now it is up to us to understand and prove the unified field. The new sciences allow us to do so in some interesting ways. Is it not possible that we do in fact experience the unified field in these ways:

- In our complete connection to our children, which is more mysterious and total than we can even imagine until we've had children?

- In our religious faiths, all of which present different versions of the unified field theory?

- And, in something Einstein hoped for but did not yet have, the kinds of technologies (PET scans, skin conductivity tracers, heart monitors) by which medical science helps us give birth to our children, tend the sick, and care for the dying?

In our glance at light, we have seen a new kind of proof for the soul, the unified field, the force that drives life. Einstein knew God, but he did not have PET scans to show him how the brain moves at the speed of light. Einstein knew, in his heart and bones, the inherent energy of the universe, but he did not have skin conductivity tests to reveal that energy, that God, *in every cell of skin*. He knew that God was part and parcel of mass but also could be separated from mass. He knew that matter worked because energy made it work. He knew that the key to unlocking the mysteries of the universe was light—the energy of matter. He just did not have the technology to prove what he knew.

Now, in the early twenty-first century, we do have the technology. Einstein was not allowed to participate in his children's births. His era did not have the soul-monitoring hospital technologies that are available now. Were he living today, though, would he not see what we have seen—that the soul is embodied electromagnetic energy; that the miracle of the compass is also the miracle of the child? Would he not extrapolate easily that, since light is light and cannot be other than light, the light of the child is the light of God? Were he living today, would he not cry, "There it is—we've learned how to watch light with technologies I never thought possible—we are seeing the unified field, the light, in the child"? You and I saw it in our children's births and have felt it as we've raised them. We've known the inherent energy of the universe in our creation of the child, just as we saw it at work on the hospital monitors.

Becoming aware of the discoveries of neurobiology, genetics, and the other new sciences has helped me wonder what Einstein would think, for these sciences have learned much from the science of physics. Einstein, as one of the geniuses of physics, would have loved our new sciences, even more as a father than as a physicist. A man of deep compassion and a devoted parent, he would see what we can see, that there is a new human evolving in our civilization, one who understands how completely everything in the universe is interwoven; and that parents, teachers, mentors, community members, know it more intimately than anyone else. This gives them—us—immense power: the power to rethink the future of humanity. We parents, and those who support us, carry civilization in our arms.

If you've ever felt stagnant as a parent or a human being; if you've ever felt that you're drowning in a sense of life getting out of control, of parenting being a race toward no real destination, of children being like worker bees you must ferry from activity to activity; if you've ever worried for your child and not known what to do; if you've ever known what to do and yet still worried endlessly—it may well be that what you have sought is what we've all sought: to feel meaningful as a parent. It may be you have sought a thinking process that will make sense of the endeavor of parenting, and thus, of our being.

Keeping in mind what we've learned in Part I, I would like to guide you in this chapter through some possible ways to change the way you think about soul, about God, about yourself, and thus about parenting and children. There is great meaning in what we do that we may not have noticed yet. We really can alter the way we think about life, and we can take a next step in our civilization. Those of us who care for children can—because of our unique experience of the soul of the child—lead the way.

THE NEW HUMAN

Cultural geographer I. G. Simmons has written of a new kind of awareness in postmodern human beings. "The core of our new environmental behavior [is] an awareness of self in which we no longer stop at the boundary of our skins nor indeed perhaps at the limit of our tentacular reach for resources. Instead we see ourselves as united with the rest of the universe in a ground of being."

The Cabala, the ancient Jewish book of wisdom, has long held that human beings are on the verge of a new step in evolution. Rabbi David Cooper, in his wonderful book, *God Is a Verb*, explains: "Just as we know that there was some kind of paradigm shift from animal consciousness to prehistoric human consciousness, and that human consciousness has gone through stages measured in various ways, such as social awareness, technological development or basic intelligence, Jewish mystics say that there is yet to come a major paradigm shift toward an entirely new level of awareness." Not surprising to those of us who study light, Rabbi Cooper, in referring to the many wisdom traditions (not just Jewish) that point to this shift, ends by saying: "All of them are designed to give us access to our inner light."

These kinds of statements ("a new consciousness is coming," and "we must follow our inner light") have served as metaphors for the human search for soul over the last few decades. They and statements like them have been pertinent to many people's life journeys and struggles. Both New Age philosophies and evangelical Christianity (which are often thought of as being contradictory) utilize much the same language, though in very different contexts. The rallies and conferences of both groups invariably feature individuals who (1) herald a new consciousness and (2) promise a path to inner light.

Evangelism (not only in Christianity but in Judaism and Islam as well) and New Age thought are evidence of the strivings of the new human: to push beyond chains that keep human thinking and feeling (the life of the whole human brain) from growing into deeper connection with the Light. Though evangelism and New Age thought provide nearly polar opposite ways of noticing that humans have evolved to make the search for the light our primary concern, we can see in them the efforts of all religions in our time: All are trying to move human consciousness toward *greater use of the human brain*—especially greater ability to sense, emote, think, and know ourselves as integral to the workings of the universe, the inherent energy of all things.

If the genius of Einstein and his colleagues who mapped light and the religious passions of our times are evidence of both the brilliance and the strivings of a new kind of human being, consider this other evidence as well.

Think back to who we were a few hundred thousand years ago, when *Homo habilis* became *Homo sapiens*; at that time, we could not experience ourselves as light, as inherent in the universe, as God. Our awareness of things is very different now, mainly as a result of modern science. We have become the very creator we used to believe was a force other than ourselves.

- Where once human beings lacked anything but instinctual intelligence, now we can not only use our native intelligence *(Homo sapiens)* but, even more, we can actually *create* human intelligence, for example, artificial intelligence. We have gone from *user* of the brain to *creator* of the brain.

- Where once we lived less than a forty-year life span, now we live at least two life spans in one. We are able to do this because we can make life-giving equipment, like artificial human hearts, we once thought only "God's intelligence" could create.

- Where once we had little control over nature's bacteria, germs, and viruses, now we have not only gained intelligence about them and learned how to combat them, but we have also learned how to actually *create* them.

- Where once we could only guess, intelligently to be sure, at the genetic composition of human beings, now we can know 100 percent of the genome, invade that composition, and even create it—clone human beings.

- Where once we could not actually see the hidden workings of the human brain, thus being forced through an intelligent self-awareness to surmise its properties, now we can look directly into the brain, and re-create it, in computer imaging, SPECT scans, and holographs.

- Where once we were not able to know what the soul is actually composed of, now we can; knowing this, we can notice how human beings join in actually creating the soul itself through their attachments to their children and to others.

Are we not in a new world? And have not the predictions of ancient wisdom traditions, like the Cabala, come true? We have reached the time in human history when we sense the infinitude of possibility for human consciousness.

If you agree that we are different now from a few hundred thousand years ago, you might also find it comfortable to say, in the free invention of the human mind, that we are a *new human*, and you might give this new human the name I have: *Homo infiniens*. I've chosen this species name with Einstein's gifts in mind. He believed we would come to a time in which infinite possibility would be the goal of human thinking. For him, the unified field was the infinite possibility he sensed, and the human's ability to prove it his goal. I think we have reached that time.

The new sciences we have explored in this book show us that the brain and self are light, and Einstein's physics showed us how infinite light is. This combination of neuroscience and quantum physics is a new science called neurophysics. A specialized science, it boldly supports the efforts of the new human. It helps us see ourselves as infinite light.

Were Einstein alive today, especially in the wake of the horrors he faced when the atomic bomb was used, he would ask us and himself this question: "Let us suppose we have, indeed, discovered a new human. What grounds this new human in reality? We have great power as human beings now. How will we determine how to use this creative power?"

You and I know the answer: The care of children is the ground of a civilization, and of the human endeavor. There is no better ground by which to measure the success of our new freedoms and possibilities than by how we care for our children. In this goal, *Homo habilis*, *Homo erectus*, *Homo sapiens*, and *Homo infiniens* are united. All put care of children above all else.

Simultaneously, the care of children is different for the new human than it was in the past, for while it can be based on *some* of the wisdom of the past, it cannot be based on *all* of that wisdom.

THE FUTURE OF RELIGION

William James, the American philosopher, said over a hundred years ago: "The human being can be thought of as a child who chains himself if he emboldens a single claim to God. He will not experience freedom until he expands the way he perceives his Maker." Expand does not mean to destroy past ways of thinking about God, but rather, to bring new wealth to these ways.

The new human is poised to do this, feeling a pressure from the new sciences and also from tensions inherent in limited visions of monotheism that intensify around the world today.

Part I of this book presented the science of the soul itself, providing you with what I hope you'll agree is a stunning proof of the existence of the soul. As that proof has taken hold of your thinking, you've been provided with a blueprint for soul development, especially from birth to adulthood, then a new way to think about a human being's mission and goals in life—a way based on what science calls "genetics" and religions have called "soul markings." This new way of thinking about life-purpose has joined with the unified field theory to expand our understanding of the inherent energy of the universe—God.

In Part II let us now explore new sciences of the soul and new ideas with specific attention to how human beings, in free invention, are expanding religion—the knowledge of God. No matter what your personal religion, I hope you'll find support and liberation in these chapters. Monotheism is still strong, and also a new unitheism is emerging—the knowledge of the unity and equivalence of energy and matter—necessitated by changes in our civilization's scientific discoveries. The changes religions are going through, which began five hundred years ago and have come to a climactic moment now, will, I hope, fascinate and inspire you to a deepening of not only your faith, but especially your care of the child. For ultimately, there is one primary reason for religion (as also for science): to provide a safe world for the child.

Not surprisingly, the last three decades, in which the development of the new sciences has taken place, have also been a time of religious tensions. All religions—whether Judaism, Christianity, Islam, Hinduism, Buddhism, or tribal and aboriginal—are in trauma today. They are filled, also, with hope borne of new approaches.

It is my contention that these new approaches very much need the new sciences; that religion as we know it is at its best when it embraces new science. This is an important connection to make, because a belief in God—the inherent guiding energy of the universe—a sense of the unified field, and a knowledge of oneself as light are ultimately useful in raising children. Children are spiritual to their core. They have not learned yet how not to be so. And studies continually reveal that children who are raised in a spiritual or religious path show greater levels of happiness than children who have little or no religion in their lives; studies show them to demonstrate fewer behavioral problems and to engage in greater moral behavior. Religion (spiritual life) is a cornerstone of raising healthy children.

But over the last decades—even centuries—a wide gulf has emerged between monotheistic religions (mainly Christianity and Islam) and twentieth-century science. Many religious people don't trust science, and scientists often claim that they must remain independent from religion in order to maintain an objective viewpoint. The new human sees all this a different way. In fact, in the new paradigm, this distrust between science and religion actually hinders free thought. It also hinders the care of children. Einstein feared the gulf between science and religion; he tried to close it. We should fear the gulf too. Ultimately, distrust between two disciplines so essential to the care of civilization and its children will lead to destruction.

The new neural and genetic sciences show us how to bridge the gulf. Great rewards await us when we take this courageous step in our civilizations, and in our homes. First, let us understand where we have come from.

Monotheism

Albert Einstein, who strove toward a new humanity, nonetheless exemplified the pure monotheism of his time. It was difficult for him to talk about God as something other than a person. "God may be sophisticated," he once said, "but he is not malicious." Einstein, a monotheist, spoke of God the way every religious person did: in the language of man, which involves separation of God, the Great, from man, the fallen.

Shema, Yisrael, Adonai Eloheinu, Adonai Echad. These are some of the holiest words in the Old Testament, a foundation of Einstein's religion and of Western culture. "Hear, O Israel, the Lord is Our God, the Lord is One." The Jews, who brought Western monotheism to humanity, were the first to make clear that there is one God and one God only: There is a unified field. Before the Jews, there were hundreds of gods by which hundreds of tribes swore, and under whose mantles they fought. Increased population required a new way of human discourse, or humans would totally destroy one another. The initial Jewish vision was a desire to unify—to bring all of humanity under one universal, omnipotent, omniscient God, and thus make peace.

In Genesis, the first book of the Old Testament, this universal God is introduced. Also introduced was the idea—one logical for that time—that the universal, perfect God was *above and separate from* the individual, flawed human being. Adam and Eve were one with God until they fell, having eaten from the tree of knowledge; their knowledge caused disunity between humans and God. The religion of Judaism, like Christianity and Islam after it (and religions elsewhere in the world) promised to teach humanity the path of reunification with God.

Not surprisingly, V. S. Ramachandran, a neurologist in San Diego, is one of the pioneers in a new field called neuroreligion by some and neurospirituality by others. He has discovered how the brain experiences both the human sense of unity and the sense of being separate from God. By using a PET scan, he has noticed changes in the temporal lobes of individuals who experience religious vision. By using a PET scan on individuals with temporal lobe epilepsy, and by watching how their body spasms affect the temporal lobes, he has noticed why this kind of epileptic feels complete unity and oneness with God. The temporal lobe, when interacting with the limbic system, is a brain center for unity.

What Einstein tried to do with the whole universe—discover the source of unity—neuroscientists like Ramachandran are doing with the brain—discovering the neural source of the *feeling* of unity. They are also showing us why, in the brain, monotheistic religion was set up the way it was: as a sacred wisdom tradition that reflects human feelings of both divine connection and disconnection from the divine.

Among Ramachandran's discoveries is this one: The human brain actually senses itself to be utterly connected, attached, and one with God, but does not feel that consciously *at all moments,* and so posits that it is intrinsically *disconnected* from the universe. In response to the sense of disconnection, the human mind creates religions, which provide the mind a way to feel connection more constantly. Though religions reflect the sense of disconnection by positing that humans are disconnected from God, they also reflect the goal of connection, by providing connection as the reward of a religious life.

Saint Augustine was a Christian teacher who taught disconnection, or separation from God, in order to teach connection. He quotes from the Psalms as he searches for the path of reunion with the separated God.

"And what is the object of my love? I asked the earth, and it said: 'It is not I.' I asked all that is in it; they make the same confession . . . 'We are not your God, look beyond us.' . . . And I said to all these things in my external environment: 'Tell me of my God who you are not . . .' And with a great voice they cried out: 'He made us.'"

Augustine did not know a completely unified field. He knew separation—the Fall, man separate from the unified field. He could not find God in the earth, nor in "all that is," nor in "my external environment." Finally, he found He-who-created-all-these-things-but-is-not-found-in-them in the idea of creation itself.

Christianity solidified the idea of the Fall—that we and all things are separate from God. Then the Islamic Koran completely absorbed the idea. It provides Muslims with the necessity of separation, then reencounter, in nearly every verse. An example can be found in Sura III, 123: "Allah had already given you the victory at Badr, when ye were contemptible. So observe your duty to Allah in order that ye may be thankful." Allah is above, we below; we are bad, Allah punishes. God, in this case, is an angry parent.

Many Eastern traditions set up the same separation of God from Man that Western traditions do (though often with less parental language) and toward the same end, to teach us how to reunify. The Bhagavad Gita, Chapter 13: "The Supreme Truth exists beyond the power of the material sense to see or to know." In the Hindu vision, there is this one Supreme Truth, the Supersoul, which is followed by material nature, and then living entities, all separate, in a hierarchy (like a hierarchy of animals, humanity, angels, then God) trying to be unified but rarely succeeding.

Is there anything inherently dangerous in the monotheistic idea that God is great and we are not; that God is perfection and we mortals are heavy with original sin; that God is higher and we lower on the hierarchy; that we just don't quite measure up to God? Is there something inherently dangerous to children when they are raised to know themselves not as God, but as fallen creatures? These are questions each of us must answer for ourselves. I do not personally teach my own children the idea of the Fall from God, though I certainly see its merit in the history of monotheism.

I cannot answer the question of religious values for you, but I can present another way of looking at God and the human, one both echoed in the neurophysics Einstein fathered and on something else hidden, we can now notice, in every world religion.

Unitheism

Monotheism is a generous religious system for *Homo sapiens*. It will be with us for many millennia, a moral anchor, and a guide to soul development.

Deep inside it there are hidden wisdom traditions that joined in all the greatness of monotheism but did not join in the idea that we are fallen, or separate, from God, the Light. These traditions assumed that all life and death were united in a unified field.

Unitheistic traditions—such as Cabalic Judaism, Sufi Islam, and Gnostic Christianity, as well as Zen Buddhism and Vedic Hinduism—assume the *sameness* of the human and God. Unity is the basis of life and of consciousness and of all things. There is no separation. In these traditions, even death, the ultimate separation, is really an illusion; and the words *enlightenment* and *illumination* are used to express the foundational experience of the universe. In these traditions, stories like that of Adam and Eve, and indeed all words, holy and profane, are metaphorical analogies of the unity that is omnipresent; they are not to be taken literally, not to be distended into a belief that God is a father (or a mother) who is angry with us, or a Being separate from us, or the Maker who places the soul in us and then will take it out.

Jewish Cabalist Moses Cardoveros presents the following unitheistic version of Judaism: "Each of us emerges from Ein Sof (the Unnameable One) and is included in it. The fact that we sustain ourselves on vegetation and animal life does not mean that we are nourished on something outside of it. This process is like a revolving wheel, first descending, then ascending. It is all one and the same, nothing is separate." Jewish mysticism is well hidden in the Psalms, and in the Song of Songs. It came to its most popular peak during the Hasidic movement in Europe in the eighteenth century. Contemporary Jewish liturgy, while clearly monotheistic, remains highly influenced by the joy tradition of the Old Testament, the Zohar, and the Hasids, gaining many of its songs from Hasidic melodies.

In 900 A.D., the Sufi mystic Abu Yezid cried, "Verily I am God, there is no God but me." Another Sufi, Husein al-Hallaj, said, "I am He whom I love . . . I am the truth." So frightening were these views to the religious authorities of the times, that these men were persecuted for them. Al-Hallaj, for instance, was burned alive by traditionalist Muslims.

Christian mystics, especially the Gnostics, hold that Jesus was a unitheist and that when he said "I am the Way, the Truth, and the Life," he was really saying "I am God, the One Light," and he meant to say it for everyone, not just himself. Monotheistic Christianity tends to interpret this kind of statement with a narrower brush, asserting that it is fine to say Jesus is God but not to say that anyone else is. There is, however, a long tradition of Christian mysticism (existing to this day in creation spirituality) which holds the unitheistic view of Christ.

The medieval Christian Meister Eckhart, who is a source of great inspiration to modern Christian mystics, wrote: "The Ground of God and the Ground of the human Soul are one and the same." And: "The eye with which I see God is the same eye with which God sees me." The Christian Saint Catherine of Siena wrote of God in a unitheistic way: "My Me is God, and I do not recognize any other Me except my God."

Saint Bernard wrote, "In those respects in which the soul is unlike God, it is also unlike itself."

Christian mystics have, until this century, had a hard go of it. The Inquisition specifically hoped to eradicate this mystical tradition.

In the Hindu tradition, we find Shankara, in the ninth century, writing: "The wise person is one who understands that the essence of Brahman (God) and of Atman (soul) is Pure Consciousness, and who realizes that they are One." The famous Vedantict words *tat tvam asi* have been interpreted by the Vedantists this way: "I am in the east and in the west, I am below and above, I am this whole world." Unitheism is interwoven with monotheism more completely in the Hindu world than in the West, though religious wars between monotheists and unitheists have prevailed for millennia in India.

In Taoism and early Buddhism, we find the loud utterance of a unitheistic approach. Chuang-Tzu wrote: "Do not ask whether the Tao is this or that; it is all things." The Zen tradition, which posits no God at all but simply sees all as One, is the most uniformly unitheistic tradition in the East.

Ralph Waldo Emerson, an American thinker who lived in the eighteenth century and was influenced by both Eastern and Western unitheism, was famous for his intuitive sense of the self as God. "I am part and parcel of God," he wrote, declaring no separation between his human soul and the Oversoul.

These are some examples of the unitheistic view that has existed for the length of recorded religious memory. It was never the mainstream view, and it was often persecuted; but now, in an era of free thinking, unitheism is returning. And science is ushering it back in. Not only Einstein but also many other of the twentieth century's renowned physicists searched for a unitheistic language for their spirituality. According to the Reverend William Harper Houff, "Einstein, Heisenberg, Schrödinger, de Broglie, Jeans, Planck, Pauli, Eddington—these are the names associated with modern theoretical physics. And every one of them wrote of his mystical proclivities." Schrödinger wrote to a friend concerning that friend's relationship with God: "What justifies you in obstinately discovering the difference between you and someone else when what is there is clearly the same?"

These physicists sensed something, just as Einstein sensed a unified field. The theologian, Dean Inge, wrote in 1926: "The centre of gravity in religion is shifting from authority to experience." In realizing this he noticed that millions of people were beginning to not only "believe in God because they went to church," but *experience* God as a completely human possibility. They sensed what we now have seen for ourselves, as we've proven the existence of not only the light that the soul of the child is, but also the infinite light that provides the inherent energy of the universe. It is 2002, and we not only have access to millennia of religion but we have also taken a step toward a unitheistic view. While the new sciences provide proof of the monotheistic idea of Shema, the singularity of God in the universe, the unified field, they also go further, into the hidden unitheism available to humanity. We can now say: *God is light and we are light, so there is never a disconnection. We are unified always.* Buddhists hint at this when they say, "You are already enlightened. Your job is just to realize it."

Are we not, in coming to this realization, closing the gulf between religion and science? Fritjof Capra's *The Tao of Physics* provided this possibility as regards physics and religion. In his wonderful book he showed the similarity between what religions have said for millennia and what physics has said for the last two centuries. In Part I we have already done this with regard to neural sciences. We have understood that there is an immense commonality between what the new sciences and the old religions know.

For this commonality to rule the day, we will have to give up, in our thinking, our idea of separation—the monotheistic idea that God and humans are not quite in sync; that God is more important in the world-scheme than humans, and humans than animals and plants; that the lack of the God/Man connection is the core of human life and is ameliorated only by conversion to a certain religion, or a certain way of thinking.

We will have to notice—whether we are monotheistic, unitheistic, or agnostic—the light that is right before our eyes. Light is light. There is no credible principle of physics by which one light is better, bigger, more important, or more complete than another. The speed of light is the speed of light. Energy is mass/volume squared. We are this. We are the speed of light, we are the equivalence of energy and mass/volume. Not only do religion and neurophysics show us this, but our love of our children, to which we eternally return, is our final proof. Every parent knows what it means to know no separation. We know it in our attachment to the children we raise. The basic unity of the universe lives completely and freely in every home.

What happens to the gulf between religion and science when we think this way? It disappears. The "Fall" (we used to be whole and loved, sparks of light in God's garden, but then we did something wrong, fell away, and became separate) is the piece of monotheism that the new sciences argue against. They show us that we are God, and always have been, and always will be. We are the light itself.

Monotheism is challenged over the next decades to adjust to the new sciences, and to absorb more of the very unitheistic content that is part of its original legacy. As the new bio- and neuro-sciences become an integral part of the life and thinking of the new human during this new century (just as physics, chemistry, and astronomy did in the twentieth), we will see not a tossing out of the great monotheistic ideas, nor of their ethical wisdom about the care of children, but we will see a tossing out of elements of monotheism that are dangerous. For instance, the justification of violent parenting, via use of the Old Testament, won't stand the test of the soul. Simultaneously, we will see an increase in the idea that God is us and we are God. This view will drive our religious teachers to alter some monotheistic interpretations of sacred texts.

We might find that priests and ministers will look at Jesus' words "I and the Father are one" in a different way, now realizing that he could not have meant that only himself, Jesus of Nazareth, and God were one; he must have meant that he, as every person, and God, are one.

Each religion in its own way will have to deal with the new reality that both physics and neuroscience have brought us. The only remaining question is not if the religions will respond but when; each can postpone the inevitable, but not forever. A new human is emerging, borne of the free invention Einstein envisioned.

BRIDGING THE GAP BETWEEN SOUL AND BODY

For the care of children, perhaps the most profound innovation that the new human will provide, through a rethinking of past doctrine, is the union of soul and body. We have seen that the soul grows in direct connection with what the body experiences. We have seen that the body carries the marks of the soul. The basic unity of energy and matter has been clarified by neuroscience, but it is hard to make the leap in thinking to a complete soul/body connection, for our sense that the soul and body are split and separate is the result of thousands of years of religious language.

Let us now, however, for the sake of our children, rethink this language. Soul and body have been separated in our religious thinking so that body could be seen as inferior and soul as superior, body as temporary, soul as permanent, soul as godly and body as sinful. Let us mature our view. Given what we've learned about the soul, there is another way to interpret, for instance, the language about soul in the Jewish Talmud Berakhoth.

"My God," says the Talmud, "the soul which thou hast placed within me is pure. Thou hast created it; thou hast formed it; thou hast breathed it into me. Thou preservest it within me; thou wilt take it from me, and restore it to me in the hereafter. So long as the soul is within me, I offer thanks before thee, Lord my God and God of my fathers, Master of all creatures, Lord of all souls. Blessed art thou, O Lord, who restorest the souls to the dead."

At first glance, this appears to say that human procreation made my body, but God breathed into that body my divine soul. Soul and body are separate.

But if we take literalism out of the interpretation—in other words, avoid thinking of God as a separate being but rather as the inherent energy of the universe—energy and matter can be unified here. The prayer to "My God" and "O Lord" are, thus, linguistic conventions. The true feeling of faith, of soul, of body is a singular feeling of unity.

In the Far East, the foundational religious text, the Bhagavad Gita, tells us: "When the body is freed of all passions, the soul is purified." This language, too, makes us think at first glance that soul and body are separate. Hinduism generally is interpreted as saying that the soul is real, the body an illusion. Yet if we understand the sentence as an early form of human language, we can see that unity is inherent in it; soul and body are completely inter-dependent.

THE FUTURE OF THE CHILD

Why is it important to make this effort? Why, indeed, spend time reinterpreting the language of religion to point out that soul and body are one, or that I and God are one? Isn't this all very intellectual? Isn't this all a "theological argument" that is of little worth to those of us raising, directly and intimately, the next generation of children?

As I have come to understand both quantum physics and neuroscience, from my vantage point as not only a professional but also a religious man and a devoted parent, I have come to understand that in the life of the child there is, in fact, *nothing* more important than bridging the gulf between soul and body. *The depth of our efforts as parents depends on it.*

Here is what I mean.

If soul and body are not one, then the body can be beaten by parents and others. The body is unimportant, after all, or an illusion.

If soul and body are not one, then the child can be physically neglected.

If soul and body are not one, then the child can be emotionally and morally undernurtured.

If soul and body are not one, then a mother will drink alcohol while carrying a baby. She is not spiritually entranced by the oneness of child and self—she has little incentive to give up alcohol.

A father will abandon his family. He does not realize his intricate connection to them.

A parent will smoke in the vicinity of children.

Grandparents will assume that the care of children is someone else's job. After all, these kids are "not my kids, I'm just the grandparent."

A society will neglect to put the needs of parents above all other social needs. Until a society realizes the fundamental unity of child with all things, a society and its values will not put parents first.

Children will be raised to become mainly economic interns, whose primary goal as adults is to make money. The gentle and subtle human search for happiness will be neglected.

Ultimately, if soul and body are not one, the joy of parenting, and the joy of being a child, will vanish, for children will become success objects, or a way mainly of fulfilling a parent's unresolved life.

We will forget that the life of the child is holy. So many people today already have.

But if, on the other hand, we understand that soul and body are one, we live differently. We can truly understand how the new sciences teach us the following about the true life of the child:

- The child is light.

- Our intuition of love and attachment is the core truth of our lives.

- We can and must understand our children—their brains, bodies, and spirits—far better than we do.

- Our constant nurturing presence, as well as the presence of many others around our children, are the sun and soil the child needs.

- Everything we do has a consequence on the basic light of the universe.

- In the beginning and the end, our work in raising our children is holy.

Given the inherent vulnerability of an infant, toddler, or adolescent, there is nothing more holy than to care for a child.

When we come to a deep understanding of the basic unity of the universe, and our participation, as parents and children, in the inherent energy of the universe, we come to think of old dualities differently. We notice, for instance, that nature and nurture are not in opposition; as human beings, we are aspects of nature who nurture, through our children, nature itself. We also yearn for the spiritualization of society (the subject of Chapter 6), in which boundaries between church and state are quite strong, but where spiritual growth (soul growth) is protected above all else in the individual life of the child. And when separation between oneself and the divine evaporates, subjectivity and objectivity evaporate, as does the fear that comes from our separation of life at death.

"*Lo hayah mavet me-olam*" (Death has never existed) says the Hebrew Zohar. Could this actually be true? In Chapter 1, we mentioned polylogical thinking, where seemingly contradictory thoughts can have equal rectitude. It is through polylogical thinking that we realize how, simultaneously, the soul and the body are one, *and* the soul can exist without the body. As we gather understanding of how light not only *is* the child, but in fact grows and changes *as* the child, we use polylogic. So it is with life and death. Death exists, but it also does not.

When my best friend, Mike Garvey, died at eighteen, I still felt his presence. The light that was my friend was no longer refracted in matter, for matter had been so shocked as to expel it; but the light he was, "a ghost" or "a spirit" in our common language, or what psychics like James Van Praagh and John Edward call "channels," or what millions of people experience as "angels," may remain in the air after death, in refraction with the material the light knew so well. To see this neurophysical possibility, we need to use not monologic, which can only see one thing at a time, but polylogic, which understands human individuality as both a matter of form and of formlessness, and of ultimate unity.

As this book began, I asked you to think differently in order to see the soul. In this chapter, I have asked you to think differently *after* having seen the soul. We have explored some of the key ideas Albert Einstein himself would enjoy rethinking if he lived now and were armed, as a parent, with the new technologies, the new science, and the knowledge of the soul of the child we now have. Thinking of ourselves alongside one of the prophetic geniuses of our century has been, I hope, not only inspiring—he is very good company—but also a kind of internal guide to our efforts here. We have explored ideas that he himself pondered late in his life—changes in thinking he himself tried to make but could not because of a lack of the neural knowledge we now have. How lucky we are to have arrived at a portion of human history when we have the freedom to rethink separation from God and understand—whether in religion or neurophysics—the existence of the unified field.

God is the child. This is the title of the final chapter of this book. To fully understand this notion of God, we are taking a journey with one more place to stop: the area of soul retrieval.

What happens to the souls of children and adults who are

traumatized by those who do not know soul and body as one and, thus, specifically damage the human soul? What happens to the light of the child? What happens to the damaged child's portion of the unified field? Why do damaged children seem "lost"? And how can they retrieve themselves? If we are saying "I am God," we must also be saying that when a portion of the soul is lost, then a portion of God is lost.

Is this true?

5

SOUL RETRIEVAL: THE PERSONAL JOURNEY BACK TO THE SOUL

The pieces of life lie scattered across the landscape of existence. Only a recovery of a deep sense of inherent order and wonder can bind up the brokenhearted.

—JAMES ASHBROOK AND
CAROL RAUSCH ALBRIGHT

The woman who entered my office that day wore jeans and a silky white shirt. Her short blond hair hung down both sides of her long face. She had deep blue eyes, surrounded by blue wire-rimmed glasses. There was a concentration of makeup beneath her eyes, where I could still see the residue of swelling from lack of sleep and perhaps from tears. A tall, thin woman who carried burdens in her slightly slumped shoulders; Lori had married thirteen years ago, at twenty-five, and now had two children.

Very articulate, though a bit shy at first, Lori confessed to me that she was depressed and might need therapy, but just wanted to meet with me this one time, to see what I thought. She had seen her minister, who felt she was severely depressed, suggesting she look into medication.

A woman who prayed daily, she expressed her distress in spiritual terms.

"I've lost myself," she said. "It's as if I'm empty inside, as if my soul is gone." Further into our session she said, "I just feel dark all the time. There's no light in my life." And so poignantly: "I feel like a lost soul, like I'm dead." In tears, she confessed, "I can't see a light at the end of the tunnel."

That Lori suffered from severe depression was very clear in the first session. Immediately, I quizzed her on her habits—was she drinking, for instance—her sleep cycle, her hormonal cycle, stresses in her life, past traumas. At the end of the first session, I referred her immediately to a psychiatrist who could get her on a medication schedule. And we set up an appointment to meet in a few days. We went over her family relations, who her allies were, and I made sure we covered the essential protocols for a potentially suicidal client.

When she came in for her next appointment, she appeared very much the same—still quite depressed. She had met with the psychiatrist, with whom she had agreed to let me consult. I felt some relief to see that required and necessary elements were in place to help provide medical and logistical support to this client who was in real pain.

And now it was time to explore, through both words and nonverbal cues, what Lori thought were some of the psychological and social elements in her depression. Over the next few weeks, I learned a great deal of Lori's life story.

Her husband Carl, she told me, was having an affair. She felt that Carl's work as a lawyer should not be keeping him out overnight like it was. Her mother was dying, her father had died a year before. Her own part-time work had come to an end, leaving her feeling listless, especially now that her children were in school all day. She had been seeing an ob/gyn for problems in her hormonal cycle (her periods came every fifteen to eighteen days).

And what of her childhood, I asked her? I learned that her mother had been cold to her, and her father was rarely around. An alcoholic—kind when not drinking, but a "berater," in her words, when he drank, "he was one of those mean drunks." She described him as a man who beat his children, then felt terrible after he sobered up. He drove a long-haul truck, so he was gone for weeks at a time.

"His being gone was a relief," Lori said, "but I missed him too. He was very affectionate to me. It was mainly my brother he would hit."

Her mother, Lori told me, was a lonely woman with low self--esteem. She had moved away from her parents and family of origin for reasons Lori still didn't fully understand, but her mother always seemed lonely without them. She was very quiet in public, very shy. She had a temper at home, but mainly she did not provide much emotion either way—happy or sad, intense or passionate.

"I know she loved me and Peter [her brother]," Lori said, "but she just didn't show it a lot."

Over the weeks, as I listened to Lori's life story, I felt immense sympathy for her. Then, later, I felt the same for her husband, who came into therapy. Carl had, indeed, been having an affair; he was the child, also, of a troubled family; in his case, his stepfather had sexually molested him for a year.

Lori and Carl saw me for just over a year. Both of them told me, many times, how desperately they wanted to work things out so their children could have a good life.

Lori said, "I don't want my kids suffering like I did. I don't want them to feel lost."

Carl said, "My kids are everything to me. I would die if I lost them."

As the weeks passed, it became very clear that both Lori and Carl, and also their two children, were moving through an immensely dark time. Lori's depression and Carl's acting out were caused by many stresses, especially the despair of terrifying childhoods that had been held over in the souls of these adults. The children were depressed and acting out too, as is often the case when parents feel they have lost their own souls.

THE SCIENCE OF LOST SOUL

Neuropsychology is the "science of lost soul." What do we mean by these words?

Since the pioneering work of Sigmund Freud, the science of psychology has been in large part about how the drives, dreams, and traumas of childhood affect the adult (and thus, society). As we have noticed in neurochemistry and neurobiology, what happens when we are a baby, or a little girl or boy, or even an adolescent, affects us forever. For Freud, the most fruitful area of emphasis was the complexities of the mother-child, the father-child, and the father-mother relationships; for every scientist of the mind since, there have been specific childhood relationships, issues, and traumas that can result in much of an adult's psychological burden. And, of course, there have been specific childhood joys as well, which when remembered by the adult, bring a sense of renewed childhood, happiness, and peace.

The field of neuropsychology adds a new area: the *biotechno-*

logical study of the brain itself. Via PET and SPECT scans, and via other indicators of brain growth and development, this new science helps people, like Lori and Carl, who have lost their souls. Neuropsychology, in moving through and then beyond traditional psychology, studies the light of the suffering adult as if under a microscope. Peering directly into the brain, we can see what psychologists used to surmise: When a person feels lost, the soul of the child, and the soul of the adult—the light of the mind—have indeed been, to some extent, lost; and, with effort and some mysterious grace, they can possibly be retrieved.

What Is Lost Soul?

The gospel song "Amazing Grace" carries these lyrics to our hearts:

Amazing grace, how sweet the sound
That saved a wretch like me;
I once was lost, but now am found
Twas blind, but now I see.

In this religious statement, a soul is lost, like a ship lost on the ocean, but by the love of God, it is recovered; that same soul lives in the darkness, but by the love of God, its sight too is recovered.

The Hindus tell the story of a boy who is lost in the dark; blind in the pitch-black dark, he calls out helplessly. No help comes. Finally, he quiets down. Now, in the complete silence, he hears a voice whisper, "You have been lost, but now you can return home." This is the voice of Brahman—God. Now he understands: In silence, one regains sight, the experience of light, and the feeling of belonging in the universe (home).

In all world traditions there is the idea that the subtle soul we are can wither, can falter, can be lost. We can feel empty—not the healthy emptiness of the Buddhist, the emptiness of no-thought, but the emptiness of the soup pot, into which we stare, famished for nourishment. We can feel lost in the wilderness—not like Jesus, who wandered the wilderness for forty days in order to learn the truth, but like a child of two or three for whom the wilderness is terrifying.

In the religious metaphors of lost souls are hints of the neuro-psychological science of lost soul. In Lori, who says, "I feel like my soul is gone," we find darkness on the brain; neuropsychologists find "dark spots" on the four lobes at the top of the brain. Furthermore, there is often decreased electric firing among neural pathways between the four lobes and the limbic system; and there is decreased neurotransmission throughout the brain. The "darkness on the brain" becomes a kind of vicious circle between brain and body. When the brain is under a prolonged neural stress, the nervous system might not fire with normal electric current (or, in some cases, can overfire in specific ways and neglect firing in others). This bodily response, in turn, keeps the brain off-kilter as well.

Daniel Amen has shown us what the darkness on the brain looks like. He has taken pictures of the brains of people who have experienced exactly what religious words, like those in "Amazing Grace," point to: These brains show "dark spots," or *lost soul*.

In his book *Firestorms in the Brain*, Amen talks about a child he was counseling—Charles—who reported that his anxieties and problems stemmed from his parents fighting every night. Amen understood that Charles's cortisol levels were unusually high—he was under deep stress. In order to help, Amen turned his attention to Charles's parents, Bob and Betsy, learning quickly that they had a very conflictual marriage. After nine months of little gain in counseling, Amen decided to apply a SPECT scan simultaneously to both Bob's and Betsy's brains (it is a very easy process, which causes no pain). Now he was able to discover the "dark spots" and give aid.

He discovered that when Bob tried to concentrate on what Betsy said, his prefrontal cortex nearly completely shut down. He could not pay attention, so he picked conflicts—fights—with her to keep himself stimulated. Betsy also had an unbalanced flow of neurochemistry—too much flow in the cingulate gyrus—which made her go over and over problems in her mind, with decreased flow in other centers in the brain.

Amen put the couple on medication, and within weeks, their lives, and the life of their child, was completely different. Amen writes, "To my delight, with their brains working in more normal ways, they were able to utilize the marital therapy work we had been doing. They spent regular times together, agreed on their parenting strategies, and even resumed making love on a more regular basis. And as Betsy and Bob did better, so did Charles."

Daniel Amen is one of those neuropsychologists who goes right to the soul of the conflict in a child's life. He finds the darkness and brings—not only through medication but also through other means as well—light back to the life of the child and the family. His work has inspired my own work with families. As much as possible, I suggest that individuals with chronic problems get SPECT or PET scans in order to see, with some exactness, their areas of neural vulnerability, of lost soul.

All of us who are interested in neuropsychology, all professionals in this field who see darkness on the soul and try to bring light, find ourselves focused not only on *where* the darkness occurs in the brain, but also on *how* it occurs. How, in the song "Amazing Grace," did that soul actually get lost? How did the Hindu boy become blind?

As we have already noted, the discovery of *how* begins with the neuropsychology of stress. The most common way our souls become lost or blind is through prolonged trauma that increases cortisol levels (stress hormones), which increases adrenaline, and thus affects nearly all aspects of normal brain development, especially development of pathways from the limbic system (where emotions begin their processing) to the four lobes at the top of the brain (where thought occurs). Invariably, some person or persons attached to the child have not understood that soul and body are one, have not remembered (or been capable of acting on the memory) that the child is God, and have done some form of damage to the child.

While neuropsychology has found that even a fully formed adult brain—limbic and neocortical systems no longer growing—can experience the loss of soul from trauma (for instance, a soldier can get post-traumatic stress though he is an adult), it is still useful to notice that most of this highly debilitating post-traumatic stress occurs previous to full brain development. For instance, soldiers who are eighteen, nineteen, and twenty years old are more likely to experience post-traumatic stress from imprisonment in a POW camp, or from seeing comrades slaughtered, or from engaging in painfully destructive acts of war, than are middle-aged soldiers and commanders.

As we noticed in Chapters 2 and 3, when a soul is traumatized for a prolonged period in childhood and adolescence, it recedes. Areas of the brain become "cold," thus the person seems to become cold. As the soul of this damaged child continues to mature, it experiences its own lack and the shame of its own lack continually, and tries to re-create that lack in others—hurting others, trying to weaken or destroy others. If the trauma has been profound enough, the soul becomes engrossed in the darkest of dramas—the will to destroy everyone else who encounters this lost soul.

THE SCIENCE OF SOUL RETRIEVAL

Each of us has sensed lost soul in ourselves or in others. We have noticed "too much ego" in ourselves or in others. We've sensed "something's not right with him." We've thought, "She's become so dark, so despondent." We are like light sensors, watching patterns of light in others. Each of us can sense lost light and yearn to retrieve it. We have felt like a person who holds a dark candle in her hand and yearns for the flame to rise again. We turn to medicines, practices, religion, and find therein the science of soul retrieval.

The science of soul retrieval today—by which light's natural, balanced pattern is retrieved—combines traditional medicines like antidepressants with different theories of psychology, alternative practices and medicines, religious practices, and neuropsychiatry. Human beings, in concert with mentors in the human community—doctors, priests, and others—strive to recover and retrieve soul that is lost in childhood or through adult traumas. When Lori and Carl sat in my therapy office, they were involved in the science of soul retrieval—mainly through the sciences of psychology (insight therapy) and pharmacology (medication). When a hardened criminal becomes a born-again Christian in prison, he and his mentors are involved in the science of soul retrieval. When an alcoholic sits, three or four nights a week, in an AA meeting, this too is soul retrieval. The brain changes its activities, redirects processing.

The alcoholic, free of the neurochemistry of alcohol intake, can attend to moral inventories and create a prayerful, centered life. This becomes possible because the chemicals in alcohol are no longer darkening the electrical processing of the brain. A hardened criminal's neural processing is refocused, through hours of Bible reading, away from "dark thoughts" in the temporal lobes, toward moral thoughts in the frontal lobes. A married couple, struggling with depression, sex addiction, and other traumas, refocuses the neurotransmission in the male brain away from inappropriate sexual urges occurring in sexual centers of the brain, and also refocuses the neurotransmission in the female brain, with the help of a serotonin reuptake inhibitor.

The field of neuropsychology shows us that if a brain system can remain refocused for a prolonged period of time, it is possible to redirect neural processing in an ongoing way. Thus a patient can, after say a year, get off Prozac but find her mind "changed" a little. She has recovered soul. After years of leading a religious life, the criminal can find another way; he can recover soul. With continued treatment, the sex addict can control himself. Neuropsychology finds the possibility of altering neurotransmission and, thus, soul. Can the depressed patient, the criminal, or the addict remain forever in the neural condition of soul recovery? Often he or she cannot. Things start to go bad again. But often soul recovery does last.

Soul Retrieval Techniques

Neuropsychologist Andrew Newberg begins his book, *Why God Won't Go Away,* with the story of Robert.

"In a small, dark room at the lab of a large university hospital, a young man named Robert lights candles and a stick of jasmine incense; he then settles to the floor and folds his legs easily into the lotus position. A devout Buddhist and accomplished practitioner of Tibetan meditation, Robert is about to quiet the constant chatter of the conscious mind and lose himself in the deeper, simpler reality within. It's a journey he's made a thousand times before, but this time, as he drifts off into that inner spiritual reality—as the material world around him recedes like a fading dream—he remains tethered to the physical here and now by a length of common cotton twine."

Newberg reveals the reason for this unusual situation. He and Dr. Eugene d'Aquili, his longtime colleague, are waiting for Robert to tug the twine. When Robert does so, Newberg and d'Aquili will know that he has entered the transcendent peak of meditation—the moment in which he "suddenly understands that his inner self is not an isolated entity, but that he is inextricably connected to all of creation." Newberg and d'Aquili have Robert hooked up to SPECT cameras by which they are trying, in their words, to take a "photograph of God." By this they mean they now have the technology to see what happens in the brain when it is "understanding the inner self," "reaching a state of spiritual or religious union," and "experiencing the timeless."

Newberg and d'Aquili are pioneers in this kind of neuropsychological research. They have been able to actually photograph what happens in the brain when it goes through soul retrieval experiences. They've learned many things about how the soul retrieves itself; one in particular is quite interesting. If you remember the song "Amazing Grace," you'll remember that the soul is lost and blind before the experience of grace, then is found and can see.

Newberg and d'Aquili have discovered that in soul retrieval, the human brain exactly re-creates this pattern. The brain "loses itself" in order to find itself. It blinds a part of itself in order for another part to see.

The soul retrieval techniques of prayer and meditation are a good example: The orientation-association area of the parietal lobe disconnects from sensory apprehension of physical space. In other words, whereas before meditating, Robert's parietal lobe was filled with normal electrical activity, during meditation it is not. It goes dark. Sensory links to Robert's orientation in physical space diminish. His ability to see his world (and see it through not just vision but also the other senses) is curtailed. He is both "lost to the world" and "blind to it."

But through this loss and blindness come gain and seeing. Robert "sees God" (bliss, transcendence), which in turn brings renewal of the soul and new vision. Newberg, d'Aquili, and their colleagues have used SPECT scans on people of many religions during their soul retrieval and soul renewal events. They found the same brain pattern. Franciscan nuns, who utilize Christian prayer rather than Buddhist meditation, nonetheless show the same type of brain functioning. After spending a number of years studying the minds of people in soul retrieval, and after discovering alterations in not only the parietal lobe but also the temporal, as well as many other parts of the brain, Newberg, d'Aquili, and their colleagues concluded: "Spiritual experience, at its very root, is intimately interwoven with human biology. That biology, in some way, compels the spiritual urge."

In this second statement is great richness. We can sense in it the truth we have experienced when we've sought to retrieve soul in ourselves—when we've engaged in therapy, gone out into nature, focused not on things that hurt but things that bring hope, gone on a much needed vacation, or involved ourselves in myriad activities that renew our souls. We "leave the hard world behind in order to find ourselves," and we sense that our urge to do so is interwoven with our hidden nature.

Indeed, soul retrieval techniques work because we meld them with our own nature. They are not alien to us; they somehow, and inextricably, fit who we are. Sometimes it's hard at first to make the techniques work—Robert and the Franciscan nuns have spent years learning how to most effectively meditate and pray—but with patience, we can learn how to retrieve soul.

Often, without our realizing it, our soul retrieval technique leads us to a regaining of innocence. William Wordsworth, the English poet, wrote this famous line: "The child is father of the man." We as adults want back the soul of the child in ourselves. We want to return to the child, who is our real self. Neuro-psychology has given some scientific truth to this idea. The parietal orientation-association area, for instance, in the person meditating or praying, returns to a more fetal and more childlike neuroprocessing. The adult, thus, becomes like a child again. *We feel the feeling of nonseparation we had as a little loved child.* We delete personal individualization from our brain functioning for a brief period of time.

That we return to childhood innocence—childhood brain patterning—should come as no surprise to us when we think about how damage is done to the developing soul of the child. It would make sense that we, as adults, in order to find ourselves, must lose our *adult* selves for a time in order to see again. We must blind ourselves to busy *adult* life and return to the innocence of the *child's* orientation in the universe and in God. At its heart, this may be part of the magic of soul retrieval—that our own human biology is set up to allow us to regain childhood innocence.

You have probably, even on a daily basis, and without realizing it, participated in this kind of soul retrieval. Here are some soul retrieval techniques that can and do go on all the time.

A person in psychotherapy can use emotional conversation to go "deeply into her issues." The hour of targeted conversation dissociates the self from everyday reality and returns the patient to the heart of childhood (or other period of lost grace), providing the patient with insight, which affects neurotransmission (allowing the patient to "see" again). The better the therapist, the more effectively this mentor will help the client or patient move into those areas of attachment and lack of attachment that have, during childhood and adult traumas, affected the development of the soul.

When you spend a great deal of time in nature, you retrieve the soul. A new field linked to neural science, called "nature therapy," shows us this. Studies have shown that simply spending time in nature affects the way the brain works. The walk in the park, the silent retreat in the woods, a weekend hunting trip . . . these allow the soul to breath again. Neurotransmission calms down, the brain calms. The nervous system calms. Cortisol levels decrease, which allows the brain to involve itself in meditative and contemplative activity that rebuilds taxed neural networks.

And while it is important for everyone to spend time in nature, studies have shown specific neural changes in *adolescents* who become involved in what we are calling soul retrieval. In an Idaho youth ranch that is set up for youths who are hard-core offenders, improvements in behavior have occurred specifically in proportion to time spent in nature.

Physical exercise retrieves soul. Aerobic breathing that consistent exercise induces—along with increased heart rate, weight burning, and muscle building—affect the electrical energy of brain and body, thus soul. Every part of the soul—from blood to bone to dopamine in the brain—is touched by physical exercise.

Prayer and meditation retrieve soul. It is a human instinct to pray—an instinct locked in the brain stem. We feel it especially when we enter a crisis time. Inadvertently, we begin to pray. We make deals with God. Those people who claim to be atheists feel increased internal pressure to find God when they are under terrible stress. It is indeed difficult to be an atheist when you're in a foxhole under enemy fire; or when you've just lost a child (even as you yell at God, "I hate you"). Whole groups of people retrieve group soul by engaging in prayer during crisis. Even under the constant experience of death and degradation, Jews in Auschwitz prayed. As soul was being taken from them, they sought to retrieve it.

PET and SPECT scans like those done by Newberg, d'Aquili and their colleagues show us how powerfully prayer and meditation affect the soul; and we intuitively know it, because we've experienced it. The more spiritually mature we are—the better we can see and feel the workings of soul and God in our own lives—the more we realize that the effectiveness of prayer is not measured by whether God, like Santa Claus, answers our prayers; effective prayer is the prayer that helps return us to joy, a sense of freedom, good character, and a sense of belonging. If we feel lonely, prayer gives us back a sense of connection. If we feel sad, prayer helps clarify who we are.

Likewise, the more deeply we study and practice meditation, the more clearly we understand that meditation is only as effective as our ability to return to the silence, the basic Sound and Light of existence. It is in the radiant silence that we retrieve soul, experience our inherent enlightenment, and renew ourselves.

If we are a man or woman in a midlife crisis, we might look at ourselves through the lens of neuropsychology. We might ask, "In what way is this life-passage an attempt to retrieve soul?" While the person in midlife passage may do hurtful things, those things generally have to do with attempts to form attachments that will convince the midlife self that he or she is okay, belongs, is not lonely, and can feel happiness again. A man leaves his family and takes on new attachments. A woman realizes how little love she is experiencing with her mate and decides to move to a life without a mate. In both these cases, the person is seeking to navigate present attachments. The man in therapy says he must regain love and a sense of his power to love. The woman in therapy will say she must regain a relationship with herself, a relationship lost in years of constricting marriage. It seems impossible for human beings who have lost soul to seek to regain it without thinking in terms of *relationship*—attachments with children, mates, others, self, or God.

Neuropsychologists have now shown us that this "relational self" is built into our being. The brain and the body are wired for relationship; the soul is wired to measure life in circles of attachments. The depth and sincerity with which some human beings experience this wiring is often quite mysterious.

A woman in her forties became a devotee of Native American shamanic practices. She was one-quarter Blackfeet by genetic lineage but had left this tradition to live in the city and work a normal job. When she was thirty-eight, her husband died of an aneurysm. She found herself unable to concentrate and very depressed. Among the many techniques she used to try and retrieve her soul (therapy, medication, prayer) was an apprenticeship with a Blackfeet shaman (medicine woman). This shaman led her through a vision quest, in which she had a dream of three kingfishers.

Though the woman had not seen a kingfisher since her childhood, three weeks after the vision quest, she looked out her front window, and there were three kingfishers. Not only did they fly overhead, but they circled back, alighted on a bare branch of a cottonwood tree seeming to pause for breath there. The woman stared at them, and they at her; they then took off again in migratory flight.

So amazed was the woman, so physically shaken, so touched by what she saw as a miracle in her life, that she lost her despair. Her grief, like a heavy curtain, parted, and she saw again the stage on which complex but joyful life could take place. When she returned to her mentor, the medicine woman, to tell her how successful she felt in her soul retrieval, the old crone just smiled and said, "I told you so."

As the rivers flowing east and west
Merge in the sea and become one with it,
Forgetting they were ever separate rivers,
So do all creatures lose their separateness.

In these words from the Hindu Upanishads we find the ultimate technique of soul retrieval—union with God. This is the feeling that the song "Amazing Grace" refers to. This is the feeling Lori was referring to when she said, near the end of her therapy, "I feel like there is light in my life again." When we seek soul retrieval, we are seeking the experience of oneness, of seeing clearly again, of feeling saved from pain, of no longer being lost, and of being bathed in light. In seeking (and often achieving) this feeling, we are retrieving ourselves from despair, from fear, from dark spots on the brain. We are redirecting the neurotransmission of the soul, the light of the mind. As we engage in these processes of redirecting, we live in hope that each will be effective.

Hope is a generous friend but not necessarily our servant. We do not always get from it what we seek. While we have a biochemical urge to seek soul retrieval, it is common for a PET scan to show that a person has recovered soul one day and then, a year later, lost soul again. For instance, the criminal who finds Jesus, his brain filled with new light, may very well get out of prison, return to his former dangerous street community, revert to drug addiction, and lose soul again. The majority of "saved" criminals do become recidivists—they reengage in the drug, alcohol, or criminal practices that forced their cortisol and adrenaline levels up in the first place. Many others who devoted their lives to retrieving lost soul similarly fall again into the loss.

But many people do retrieve lost soul. We might pray five times a day but still suffer immeasurably; we may meditate three hours a day and still feel despair; we may take antidepressants and become burdened by the side effects; we may engage in therapy for years and feel like we've accomplished nothing at all—yet still we know that we might, indeed, retrieve lost soul. We hope, we work hard, we take medicine, we walk, we meditate, we pray. The woman who saw the kingfishers did not feel depression again after that day. Lori and Carl were able to get help and even develop a happy marriage. Lori's depression lifted. Carl's addiction-induced increase in stress hormones reversed; he decreased his addiction and decreased his stress. Some criminals find happiness in true freedom and gain a new lease on life.

When Souls Cannot Be Retrieved

I worked in a prison once with a pedophile who had been prescribed a high-dose estrogen patch. The high estrogen doses—alien to his male body and brain—made him grow breasts and become obese; they completely killed his sex drive. He was let out of prison, and as long as he continued this very invasive hormonal treatment, he did not reoffend. He understood that because of the prolonged period (five years) of sexual molestation he had experienced between ages six and eleven, his brain had been rewired toward pedophilia. He had lost soul. He understood that he must stay on his meds and his estrogen in order to mimic the retrieval of soul, and stay out of prison.

And yet his case—like the case of most high-level sexual offenders—is a case of irretrievable soul. In some cases soul cannot be retrieved; at best, soul retrieval can be imitated or mimicked. If this pedophile were to stop the invasion of treatment chemicals into his brain system—if, in other words, he disengaged from this chemical imitation of soul retrieval—the dark spots on his brain would rule his body. If we were to do a PET scan on his brain we would notice that those dark spots have not gone away—neither prison, nor medication, nor hormones can "rewire" his traumatized brain. He can only, by artificial means, imitate the rewiring.

A friend of mine, Sally Grant, a nurse in Seattle, told me a story about a man who came to the nurses' station and asked her and two of her colleagues some questions about their administrative procedures. The man wore sunglasses, and was dressed, in Sally's words, "like your average guy."

Sally told me, "But I and one of the other nurses sensed something about him, something weird. He was handsome and smooth, but we sensed something wrong. We called the cops."

By the time the police came, the man had gone. A month later, Ted Bundy was captured. Sally recognized his picture in the newspaper. He was the man with the sunglasses that night.

"It was like Carla and I could smell the evil on him," Sally said. Interestingly, her third colleague, who was very busy, "smelled" nothing. Distracted by her work, she could not attend to the hidden sensation of Bundy's evil, but the two nurses who could attend sensed it unmistakably.

Ted Bundy, like Adolf Hitler, and like the pedophile who could not survive in society without estrogen, was a person whose soul could not be retrieved. The nurses who paid attention sensed a lost, irretrievable soul. They sensed "something not quite right." They sensed evil.

In my therapy practice I worked with a woman who had been in and out of foster homes throughout her whole childhood. She developed an attachment disorder, which made it difficult for her to have a family. She had been divorced five times. After a year of therapy with me (following many years with many other therapists), as well as various other kinds of treatments—from religious activity to medications—she told me she felt that she was like an animal that should be put down: She was incurable and would just keep ruining other people's relationships, and her own.

While I told her to keep trying to find answers, and pledged my loyalty, as her professional therapist, to her process, I did believe her. She was nearly fifty and had so many different psychological disorders that I did not see much light at the end of the tunnel for her.

While hope is generous and must not be measured too frugally, stark reality is often of great value too. When a child has his or her developing soul crushed and destroyed, that child as an adult may not be able to fully retrieve the destroyed divinity. When we snuff out the light of the young child, the adult may well remain in darkness until death, like a great relief, comes to pay its visit.

The science of soul retrieval is, like any medical science, not capable of healing everyone. Knowing this—noticing that the PET scans of some lost souls do not regain all light—hopefully sobers parents and caregivers, and indeed the human community. Now that neuropsychology is an available science to us, adults can far better see the consequences of their actions on the souls of children.

THE NEW HUMAN: PUTTING CHILDREN FIRST

Child advocate Madelyn Swift, who has long studied the travails of the family in our fast-paced culture, has a beautiful phrase: "In order to retrieve our children, we'll have to retrieve ourselves." Her book, *Teach Your Children Well*, is a practical statement about how parents who retrieve their sense of balance can thereby fully care for their children.

For a few decades now, especially in the 1990s, there has been a trend toward "caring for myself" without a clear context of why we do so. The catchphrase "the Me generation" was a linguistic attempt to express this trend. "If I want it, I go out and get it." "I have to take care of number one." "I've only got myself." While many people may well have acted selfishly during "the Me generation" (and while selfishness can exist in any generation), many people during the Me generation were participating in a search to retrieve what Freud called "our radiant intelligence." Many people, in searching for a free self, were trying to answer the question: In what ways do I need to care for myself so that I can better care for the children?

We very often get the urge to retrieve soul once we have had children. "I want to do better by my kids," we say. "I want the best for my baby, so I need to work some things out in life." "Now I have no choice. I have to get healthy." Instinctively, we feel we must regain soul and "set our house in order" so that we can protect the human proclivity for relationship, attachment, and growth. The soul of the adult is different from the soul of the child in that the soul of the adult is directed toward the care of children's growth, whereas the soul of the child is directed toward growth itself. Because we know this instinctively, we seek a psychological healing of our own childhood defects.

The Hollywood actor Brad Pitt spoke to this point quite eloquently when asked why he had gone into therapy. "[It was like] taking a class on yourself. . . . I choose to talk about it because I believe if everyone did it, we'd have very few conflicts. I certainly don't think we'd be at war right now if everyone had a couple of semesters on themselves.

"I found it as something very exciting, a redirection of understanding. The other issue is this. As my wife and I begin a family, I don't want to pass on any dysfunctions, no matter how minor or innocuous they might be. I don't want to pass that disease on to my kids. I want to get as clean as I can for them."

Brad Pitt expresses the instinct we all have. The great destiny of each of us is to care, in some way, for children. It can be argued that anything—any desire, urge, infatuation, interest, problem—that takes us away from this destiny is the result of having lost soul sometime earlier in life; it can also be argued that the extent to which we retrieve soul is the extent to which we return to the ability to see the light and the soul of the child in our homes, on our streets, in our schools, and in our society.

In religious or spiritual terms, we might understand our lives this way: Spiritual maturity comes when we arrive at a life-era in which the great challenge now is not material success or ego approval, but the quieting of appetite and, through that, purification, the immersion in a holy life. In neuropsychological terms, we might say that the human being, led by the brain and other body systems, searches for meaning via a number of drives, instincts, and desires that grow from not only its genetic markers but also from its past experiences. Deep inside our neural webbing is the overarching need to (1) assure immortality through the existence and safety of the child and (2) care for the specific psychological needs of the soul's own past self (what the person experienced in childhood). Psychological maturity, in this neuropsychological model, comes through:

1. The adult's full ability to care for the child, who is known instinctively to ensure immortality and is known psychologically as the mirror of self; and

2. The adult's full ability to care for the child for reasons beyond instinct and ego-mirroring; reasons involving the full ability to protect and guide the soul, light, and holiness of the child.

While modern sociopsychology (which comprises most of today's field of psychology and is based on social observations by psychologists from Freud to the present) emphasizes adulthood as a full individualization of the human into a separated individual called "the adult," neuropsychology sees that *there is no full separation between children and adults.* The child and the adult are one in that they are comprised of the same neural and genetic material. Both are God, in unitheistic terms; both are light, in physical terms; both are united by life-process, in psychological terms.

There is a basic unity connecting all generations—generation after generation doing what it must to care for the next, adult after adult making whatever sacrifices are necessary to be fully empathic to the child. Often the needed sacrifice, like Lori's and Carl's, is the sacrifice of pain and hurt—the giving up, the relinquishment of old patterns in the mind, darkened there by childhood, and thus the retrieval of light, of true human power, by which to self-heal depression and aid a broken but loving marriage. Often the needed sacrifice is, as Pitt puts it, "a class on myself."

It should not surprise us that the field of neuropsychology, like the fields of neurochemistry, neurobiology, genetics, and neurophysics, constantly return to the needs of the child. We seek to connect with God, with light, with a Higher Power or a personal sense of power; we seek to become physically and morally healthy; we seek to free our souls to a holy life. In all this, we are like tree branches reaching toward light, reaching upward and outward not only so that the trunk will get the nutrition it needs, but also so that each individual leaf, each child, interconnected, will gain the light by which to grow.

Is it possible, then, that there is a beautiful idea waiting for us as we understand why we are alive? Is it possible that all of life—animal, plant, human—is so instinctively focused on the care of the soul of the child, that we might stretch our minds to see how God—whom we have thought of as a great Being on high—is in fact the beloved child right in our home?

This is truly a holy and generous idea. Let us finally, fully, enjoy it in the next chapter.

6

GOD IS THE CHILD: THE FUTURE OF THE FAMILY

I see God in every human being. When I wash the leper's wounds I feel I am nursing the Lord himself.

— MOTHER TERESA

Outside the window, snow fell wildly, a wind knocking the thick white flakes against the glass. Snow, in Seattle, is somewhat rare, especially snow with a punch like this snow had.

Inside the warm and cozy Sunday school classroom, twenty first through third graders gathered on a carpet with a young man who faced them seated on a tiny "kid" chair, his bottom nearly hanging over the sides. He held in his hand a book about the Jesus story, from which he'd been reading for the last few minutes. Joseph and Mary were wandering in Judea, Mary sitting on a donkey (or an "ass," as this story reader had joked a couple times, just to keep the young crowd attentive). In Bethlehem Joseph and Mary were turned away from many lodgings, but then a kindly fellow let them sleep on hay in a barn.

"It's not a barn, it's a manger!" a first grader called out.

"Okay," the reader agreed. "A manger." And he continued reading aloud. Mary went into labor that night, giving birth to a beautiful baby, Jesus. The birth of this child was heralded by a huge light in the sky, a light followed by three magi who made their way to Bethlehem. A shepherd boy watched the light from his hill. When the magi arrived, they brought gifts to the boy.

"Behold, God is born," one of the magi said, placing gold amulets in the baby's crib.

"They mean 'the *Son* of God is born,' " a second grader said, correcting the adult reader. "Christians say Jesus was the *Son* of God."

"It says, '*God* is born,' " the reader responded, turning the book around to show the students.

" 'Behold, God is born,' " the second grader read.

"I like that," a third grader smiled. "God is a kid. Like us."

"Remember," the reader reminded the children, "according to the Christian tradition, Jesus was both God *and* the Son of God. He had many names." The young man pondered aloud, "But He could be a kid, I guess. Jesus was God, and he was a baby. So, sure, a kid could be God."

"God is in everything," a second grader called out.

"God *is* everything," a third grader emphasized, his mind having a decidedly mystical bent.

"That's what my mom says too," a first grader chimed in.

"Yeah," a third grader agreed, still pondering the earlier thought. "A kid could be God."

"But then God would have to be *all* children," Mrs. Finkel, the class's Sunday school teacher, pointed out logically.

"And all adults too," a third grader said.

"Sure," another child said, twirling the hair above his right ear with the fingers of his right hand.

"Well . . ." Mrs. Finkel hesitated. "Let's be careful here."

The reader that snowy day was me, at a Jewish Conservative Temple's Sunday school in Seattle, Washington. I was in my early twenties. In my teens, I'd read books by Chaim Potok *(The Chosen, The Promise, My Name Is Asher Lev)*—books about Jews in America. I was of Jewish origin by my father's and part of mother's blood, but my parents had moved away from Judaism during my upbringing, searching for truth in many religions. As a teen, I'd discovered Potok and had found myself deeply attracted back to Judaism. I had gone to synagogue to learn Hebrew and become, in religion, what I'd been born to by blood. I successfully learned minimal Hebrew, but when I went to college, I strayed again from Judaism, getting my undergraduate education at Gonzaga University, a Catholic college, then moving to Seattle for graduate school at the University of Washington. In Seattle I began going back to synagogue again, renewing my search for my Jewish roots. On this particular Sunday, I had volunteered to read to students in the synagogue Sunday school about the Christian story of Jesus, a story about which the children already knew a great deal, from general American culture. The religious director of the synagogue felt that at Christmastime this particular year, it would be nice to talk to the students about Jesus from a Jewish perspective, since Jesus had been born (and lived his whole life) a Jew.

The words "Behold, God is born" had now started a nice little discussion among the students about who God is, and whether God—whom children generally see as a Grand Person—can have more than one "son." Judaism, a religion in which the Messiah has not yet come, always finds interesting the perspective of Christianity, in which the Messiah has not only come, but soon may come a second time.

The Jesus story, which I now finished reading for the class, seemed to light up the children's minds. They asked many questions and even answered some for themselves.

"Was Jesus really the Messiah?"

"For Christians, he is."

"God has *lots* of sons *and* daughters, not just one."

"Do Christians believe that?"

"I'm glad we get Hanukkah presents, since the Christian kids get Christmas presents."

"Yeah. Me too."

"My mom says Christmas is too commercialized."

"What's commercialized?"

I enjoyed this discussion, which Mrs. Finkel, a very traditional teacher, followed closely. I turned the children back to the earlier comment—"What about the idea that God is a child? Isn't that a neat idea?" Mrs. Finkel reminded the children that we could only mean it like it was meant in a story (metaphorically). In truth, *we* were not God. It was wrong to think of ourselves as God, for we were merely human. God is God. Children are children.

I recall this moment in Sunday school quite vividly because it was one of those moments in which I found myself making a strange, inner break with some aspects of tradition. Even as a youth, the idea that "God is a kid" made sense to me. The idea that we could not be God, for we were human, did not make sense. In my early twenties, an era in my life during which I struggled to retrieve soul I had lost during my own brutal childhood, I sought a better life through relationships, religion, therapy, higher education, and travel. As happened so often, there were hints of a happier life in religious stories; and on this particular morning, in the minds of the children themselves who listened, I had the experience of not only "hearing" an idea, but also of *feeling* it with all my soul.

Especially given my own childhood—in which I experienced significant physical abuse—I could not help sitting there and thinking: Wouldn't it have been better to feel, during my own childhood, that I was God? Wouldn't it be wonderful, and so humane, for any child to be treated with that kind of respect, devotion, and adoration? It was every child's dream, wasn't it? Perhaps it was every child's right. So why did it not happen? Why, as a human being, was I specifically *not* God? Why was it so easy for Mrs. Finkel, and me, and everyone else we knew to state, as a fact, that these kids were not God?

I recall this moment as an important one for me, and I recall my thoughts as I left the synagogue that snowy morning to catch the bus, but in retrospect, no matter its soulful power, it did not feel at the time like a moment of pure understanding. I was very young—ultimately, my mind filled and whirred with questions, not insights. I had attempted suicide once already—I was preoccupied with just trying to stay alive and trying to set a useful adult future for myself in the world of adults. Religious philosophy was incomplete for me, perhaps because I knew little yet of the sciences that provide, in collusion with religion, a foundation for my present life and work.

Yet there is a similarity among the Seattle moment, the conversation with Great-grandma Laura in Nebraska, and my daughters' births—a similarity I can see better now. In each, conventional assumptions about God and soul were challenged, in my presence, by the voices of children. In Spokane, as my hidden daughters' lights emerged on the monitors, the soul of the child became obvious. In Blair, Nebraska, the children seemed to be saying, "It's possible to know God and soul better than ever before." In Seattle, the children spoke of God the child. Now, much older, a professional and parent myself, I see the possibility that the new sciences have brought us too: We can understand God as never before.

Already in these pages, we have shown that the soul is light and light is the soul; we have seen that electromagnetic energy, on which all life depends, is the base construction of our children, of ourselves, of everything around us. We have understood that this light is God, the inherent energy of the universe. Is it not then time in our human evolution to agree that God—whom humanity has called the Lord, Allah, the Unspeakable Name (Y-hw-h), the Source, the Force—is not somewhere else far away, but right here, in our own homes, breathing?

What else in life is more important to us than our children? How can they not be God? The children in Seattle knew they were. They knew, at whatever inchoate level, that we adults are not merely raising kids—we are raising God.

This chapter proceeds with their idea in mind. We will explore how to look at our families not just as economic or "caregiving" units, but as something else too, something so inspiring that it is the seat of human meaning and truth.

GOD NEEDS US

Traditionally we have thought of ourselves as needing God and God coming through for us when we need Him.

Symeon the New Theologian, a tenth-century Christian born in ancient Turkey, tells the story of meditating one morning after feeling a deep sense of sadness and seeing, suddenly, the appearance of God. God shone like "an intoxication of light, swirlings of flame."

Symeon, no longer sad but now joyful, fell prostrate, crying, "You appeared as light, illuminating me completely in Your light. I became light in the night, I who was found in the midst of darkness." Symeon's words and experience are compelling evidence of a human being who needed God. God appeared to Symeon as needed. God answered his prayers.

The ancient Hindu *Chandogya Upanishad* suggests that people who suffer need to remember that "there is a Light that shines beyond all things on earth, beyond us all, beyond the heavens, beyond the highest heaven; that Light shines also in our world." If we will but see this light, if we can immerse ourselves in it, our troubles will be healed.

Wendell Berry, the contemporary poet and naturalist, writes of his relationship with nature, the place and God of his own healing and soul retrieval. "When despair for the world grows in me and I wake in the night at the least sound in fear of what my life and my children's lives may be," he says, he goes into nature and comes "into the peace of wild things who do not tax their lives with forethought of grief. I come into the presence of still water. I feel above me the day-blind stars waiting with their light. For a time I rest in the grace of the world, and am free."

Symeon, the ancient Hindus, Wendell Berry, each express the blessed feeling of knowing that God (nature) will comfort the lost, will inspire the retrieval of soul, will fill the mind with new ideas and graceful activities, will bring freedom to the imprisoned, will provide moral laws to civilizations, will show us all the paths of light and love we need in order to grow and find peace. In an infinite number of ways, each of us has needed God and often realized that we are finding what we need from God.

We have perhaps less often looked at God from the opposite

perspective. We have perhaps less often realized that God needs *us*. This is a more difficult idea for the human mind to grasp. And yet, right before us, is God's need. If we open our eyes, we cannot miss it.

"One hesitates to bring a child into this world without fixing it up a little," writes the contemporary poet Alta. In her words is the face of God's need. "We human beings are built into the great scheme of things in a very basic way," writes the physicist Paul Davies. Here, again, is evidence of how God needs us. "I want to do right by my children," says a client in my office. "I have to deal with my problems so that my children can have a better life."

What are all these if not evidence of God's need of each of us? Why do we fix up the world? What is our profoundest motivation? Is it not to make a better world for children? Is not God speaking volumes of need as we instinctively care for our child?

What is the purpose of the great and profound order of the universe, in which each of us is inextricably interconnected? Is not the purpose to bring the chaotic needs of the light into the care of those capable of bringing order to the light? Are we not, each of us, participating in the greatest act of respect for the most infinite of needs—the need of God to be cared for?

What is the inspiration of the adult's search for peace? What is this child who, even before he or she can speak, moves a parent to do the nearly impossible—to change a hardened, saddened mind? Are these not indications of God's great need that each of us grow, feel, care?

And on what face is God's need of us any clearer than on the face of a child? In what mystery does God's need more clearly reside than in the mysterious, yet now more easily clarified, soul of the child? How beautiful are both our religions and our sciences for showing us that God is the child, the light of all lights, and that God will no longer accept us being merely the takers but calls each of us to create a life in which we are, through care of our children, the givers. How lucky we are that God needs us as much as we need God.

The new neurosciences challenge us to understand that not only is each child "watched over by God," "God's temple," and "capable of being godly by doing good deeds"; not only is each child the inherent energy of the universe, the light of being; not only is God not merely "the omnipotent and omniscient power whom we humans need"—*God, as the child, needs us.* It is in large part the need God has for us upon which the universe is constructed. It is this need, as well, upon which families strive to create themselves.

Consider the following ways the sciences have shown us that God needs us:

- We've understood that the inherent energy of the universe leaves markings on each child's soul. Are not these markings by God the expression of how God needs us to care for the born child God is?

- We've understood that God compels each of us to retrieve soul when we've lost it. We are constantly wrestling with personal demons and angels. Is not the inherent energy of the universe restless to regain balance, and does not that energy constantly signal us to come to the aid of life itself—God's aid?

- We've learned that the inherent energy of the universe, the light that is always within the darkness, does not remain

dormant in life but tugs at us to care, to be compassionate, to grow it, like a flower. The soul grows. Why? We
are compelled by instinct to help it grow. Why? Because
soul and God need us to help that flowering occur.

Perhaps throughout human history—certainly in religious and
philosophical texts we've referred to in this book—God has shown
clear need. Perhaps we were earlier unable to fully comprehend
God's communication, but now the science of *neurobiology* shows
us how God grows and expresses need. The science of *genetics*
shows us the markings etched by divinity on the soul of the child.
In *neurophysics,* we learn a great deal about the composition of
soul. In *neuropsychology,* we understand God's pain. Through
these sciences, as in everyday life, mysteries of the universe express
themselves in the human process you and I as parents are called to
nurture: the process of raising children.

And so, as we have explored these new sciences, we not only can
understand the ways in which the soul of the child develops in your
home, community, schools, and religious institutions; but also we can
understand how clearly we are being called to gracefully manage the
development not only of our "kids," but also of *God,* in our homes.

It is a beautiful idea, to think of our children as God, and to go
even further by noticing how God needs our every breath of care,
compassion, and direction. It is an idea that this book has built
toward, and one that can, I hope you'll agree, free the soul of the
parent to a life of meaning and purpose.

The idea that God needs us is an idea which I hope will form the
bedrock of families in the future. It is also an idea that faces a large
barrier in modern life. Even with the best science before us, and
even with millennia of world religions supporting that science, a

thread runs through modern life that stands in the way of those people who recognize the soul of the child.

The Masai tribe in Africa—one of the oldest tribes on earth—have a beautiful tradition. When a person from one village meets a person from another, they greet each other with *"Kasserian ingera?"* "How are the children?" This salutation is provided even by young warriors who have no children. And even these warriors answer one another: "The children are well."

The Masai people experience little or no loneliness.

When the Masai are asked why a war or other conflagration is being fought, they traditionally answer: "For the children." The implication of all this is that the children are the seat of meaning for the Masai. Not surprisingly, for the Masai, *there is no distinction between the children and God*—all elements of life are One life.

So it is with many existing aboriginal tribes, and so it was for all of our long-ago ancestors. Until about four thousand years ago, we were very aboriginal in our thinking. Making a distinction between humans and God is a relatively new concept in human history and has led to the development of an amazing modern civilization. But it has led, also, to a terrible loneliness. Let us pause for a moment and notice the loneliness that our children experience today—in their lives, their homes, and their neurochemistry. It beckons all of us—parents, professionals, and the new human—to look more closely at the light.

THE LONELINESS OF THE CHILD

When she was ninety-four, Great-grandma Laura said to my daughters, "It's hard getting old. You're so alone." Before my daughters were born, she spoke in a strong, tempered voice. It did not carry the wavering pitch of extreme old age. She lived alone—her husband long dead—in a house on a hill in Tekamah, Nebraska, an even smaller town than Blair, which looked out over green fields toward Iowa and Missouri. She spoke aloud of social things at social gatherings—about her garden, her memories. She was a talker, a doer.

By the time she had entered the nursing home, her eyes, ears, and even voice had begun to relinquish the soul's light, her sensitivity to sound leaving her ears and the parts of the brain needed for hearing, her sensitivity to vision leaving her eyes and optical areas of the brain, and the force of her voice leaving her throat. At ninety-four and ninety-five, as she struggled to speak a few sentences to my children, her voice was barely audible, and loneliness had become her most frequent companion.

Young girls, my daughters could not yet fully imagine what Great-grandma meant by loneliness, but you and I can. As we move through adult life we understand loneliness better. It is our nature, as adults, to do so. We even remember times, as children, when we felt lonely in our own homes, neighborhoods, or schools—times when we began to realize that we were not fully in control of our lives, and human love could be fickle, and there were dangers everywhere.

For children today, the experience of loneliness has increased manifold. Our children have everything, but unlike the Masai children, they lack the sense that they are God. They experience and express this lack in various ways, from addiction, to depression, to overt violence in schools and homes. Sometimes, we keep our children—and ourselves—so busy, we don't see the loneliness of our children.

In this chapter, I will invite you to a deeper understanding of the larger adult culture in which the soul of the child is today nurtured. The culture in which we live has become a better material provider for children than previous cultures—but also a better predator. It encourages families to see children as items and economic interns, which further isolates them from human bonds. Because a society can best measure its health by how well it cares for its children, this chapter presents ways in which our society abandons the soul of the child to loneliness—in the end, we shall see that our society loves loneliness too much. That end will be our new beginning—the seat for the future of the family.

The Facts of Loneliness

When we notice that many children today are lonely, we might say, God is lonely in our homes. And it is impossible for the child to be lonely unless the adult is lonely. Because the soul of the child is by nature a relationship in progress, it does not naturally know loneliness. Physicians in the field of sociobiology call loneliness "the disease upon which all other physical and mental illnesses depend," or, as human ethologist Phon Hudkins, of the Human Ethology Institute, has put it, "the most damaging human disease." It is a sad gift given to the child from the soul of the adult.

As we've seen, the biochemistry of today's children may well be subtly but definitely changing from the biochemistry of previous generations. As attachment decreases between parents, extended family, and children, our children become more lonely, and the soul of the child changes. We've explored this stress-cortisol reality in previous chapters. Here are some facts we've learned in the last few years that show us how difficult life has become for the souls of many children.

- Teen suicide has increased 200 percent in the last twenty years. Teenagers report the highest incidence of "feelings of loneliness" (higher than elderly people).

- Over 300,000 children in the U.S. each year suffer some form of sexual exploitation, including prostitution.

- About 15 percent of American children are diagnosed with ADD/ADHD (attention deficit disorder/attention deficit hyperactive disorder). Of these children, 90 percent are boys.

- One in five girls will struggle at some point with some form of an eating disorder.

- Ten percent of children suffer from depression.

- Nearly 6.5 million Americans are in jails or prisons (this is a higher per capita incarceration rate than any other country except Russia).

- We have the *highest* per capita number in the world of young people (ages fifteen to twenty-five) in our prisons and other state penal systems.

- Researchers at Harvard University and the World Health Organization have discovered that depression costs more years of useful life in children than any other condition except respiratory and newborn infections.

Some of these statistics should really give us pause. How can it be, in a society of luxury, that so many children suffer so much mental defect?

While there are many ways to look at what is happening to our children, one way is to look, as we have, at the workings of the child's body and mind—to notice that when soul is under stress, it changes neurochemically. I hope this book has shown you that to avoid understanding this is to abandon the soul of the child.

Over the last few decades, most of us have become very conscious of how our culture abandons its children to stress. Two areas of cultural predation on children probably come immediately to your mind:

- The media overstimulates children with sexual imagery but undernurtures their emotional and character development.

- Corporations and advertisers exploit children constantly.

But does our focus on these elements of our culture fully explain our children's loneliness? Over the last two to three decades, finding fault with "culture" has been easy. Our culture is monolithic and oriented toward consumption; it is too big, we might say, to care about the individual child. It preys on the naïveté of all children. Our children see four hundred advertisements per day; it is difficult for them not to base some self-image on the cultural images presented them by profit-making institutions. Sometimes these institutions systematically poison children. The recent agreement made between tobacco companies and the federal government was a forced, court-ordered end to the exploitation of the child by manufacturers of a chemical—tobacco/nicotine—that poisons adolescent souls.

Modern psychology has focused primarily on the problems faced by children and families in a monolithic culture. It has also studied the problems of the nuclear family. After "the culture," the "breakdown of the family" is the most discussed root of our children's loneliness. Over the last few decades, finding fault with the nuclear family has also been easy. In an epidemiological study of depressive disorders, for instance, completed in a school district in South Carolina, researchers discovered that the only significant predictor of a major depressive disorder among children was lack of family cohesion. The obvious is right before us: Parents matter, and parents are having difficulty keeping up with what children need. A recent study by the president's Council of Economic Advisors discovered the stress on children created by the "time crunch" in nuclear families: In the last three decades, "parents have lost an average of twenty-two hours every week" that were once spent with children. "By the time children reach eighteen, that is more than two extra years their parents are away from home."

Culture and nuclear family are large parts of the loneliness puzzle, and our vigilance about issues that come to bear on children via cultural institutions and via the nuclear family will and must continue—the new sciences bear out the fact that both cultural institutions and the nuclear family are putting terrible stress on children.

The new sciences, however, also point to a third area of abandonment which is the least discussed today and needs to be greatly discussed: This third area has always held the key to the flourishing of a child's biology: It is the family structure we call *extended family.*

The new human, and the family of the future, will closely scrutinize a number of possible solutions to the loss and abandonment of the child's soul, but foundational among these will be the more careful utilization of extended families.

THE FUTURE OF THE FAMILY

Among the thirty cultures that I surveyed in order to check the universality of the biological research I've presented to you, I found many cultures that are relatively homogenous—for instance, in which the citizens speak mainly one language. The United States is one of these. We have, to a great extent, homogenized human life— our massive popular culture has helped do this, as have our democratic, egalitarian, and conformist views on human development. We try to help everyone live "on a level playing field," and quite often, we succeed. If individuals conform to certain marketplace rules, they can succeed. If parents raise their children toward these conformities, their children have a greater chance of social success. Japan is also an example of a basically conformist culture. In Japan, unlike the United States, there is a smaller window for adolescent rebellion, but in both, by the time adulthood sets in, most of the society has conformed to a relatively homogenized version of family, extended family, and cultural institutions. In both these countries a severe work ethic coupled with material rewards for both technological creativity and social conformity lead many individuals in both cultures to social success, and that success is the goal of family systems.

India is a different kind of country. With a population at nearly a billion people, it wrestles with different demons and different angels than do countries like the United States and Japan, which hold population in better check. Two primary differences between India and these more information-based cultures—differences that have had a great influence on both my own personal and professional life—are these:

- In India, all four stages of the development of human family systems (I'll detail these in a moment) are still present.

- In India, the extended family is obvious everywhere.

During my boyhood in the 1960s, my own family lived in Hyderabad, India. I was brought up not only by my own parents, but also by many "aunties" and "uncles." This was the natural state of affairs there. Children of thirteen and fourteen are married every day in India, bear children soon after, and the extended family raises the children. When a father (or mother) must go to another city to work, the extended family is already in place to help the children. When a parent dies (many mothers die in childbirth), grandmothers and aunties step in to care for the children.

Extended family *is* family in India. The distinction between nuclear family and extended family is often blurred, at best. The idea that the soul of the child can be successfully grown in the home of one person—a single parent, for instance—is alien to most of Indian culture. The soul of the child flowers among the many people who love the child.

Because of this, *individual identity* is seen differently in India than in the United States. An individual gains his or her identity primarily from attachment to family; social success, for most Indians, is a secondary attribute of identity.

This way of seeing the world—which, I hope you'll agree in a moment, holds insight for helping our more lonely culture—is more possible in a country like India, where the evolutionary stages of family-systems development are all still present. What are these stages?

The Four Stages of the Human Family

The new science of sociobiology (often called "evolutionary biology") has directed us to understand that not only do individual organisms evolve, but so do organic biological systems; not only does the human soul evolve, but so do the life-giving systems that care for the soul. The human family is one of these systems.

We can isolate four distinct stages in the development of the human family. It is useful to briefly outline them.

Stage 1: The Survival-Driven Family. This family system dominated most of human history. We were hunter/gatherers until about ten thousand years ago. We existed as subsistence and *survival* groups. Our extended families (tribe) existed to make possible the survival of the child to adulthood, and the survival of the adult to about a forty-year life span.

Among hunter/gatherers, populations were low, resources could be discovered if each tribe remained somewhat nomadic or if a town was settled near a river or an ocean. Social ethics inherently followed from the difficulty of life, under the authority of a few medicine men and women and other elders. The authority of these few was considered divinely marked or spiritually earned, and attacks on their authority were rare. People did what they needed to and what they were told to by their leaders.

Stage 2: The Morality-Driven Family. As agriculture took over human development ten thousand years ago, populations increased exponentially. Millions of people were born every year, and because of agricultural innovations, far fewer died. Because there was now a greater pool of human individuals available, diverse human qualities developed, especially variety in areas such as worldview and behavior. Human life became somewhat out of control—especially in areas of war-making among groups and tribes. Higher population density required more monolithic power bases for moral and behavioral development. Greater resource availability meant that human beings could do more than survive—they could thrive. Stronger civilizations set out to bring their monolithic worldviews to smaller civilizations (somewhat like corporate takeovers today). Groups conquered groups, and nation-states began to form.

Family systems during this time became *morality driven*. The Old Testament, the New Testament, the writings of Confucius, the Tao Te Ching, the Bhagavad Gita, then the Koran and most other seminal religious texts guided civilizations and families in how monolithic life (life run by governments and social institutions) should be lived. Day-to-day rules were set forth. Families managed their care of the child within these rules. Societies and families put morality—the control of human behavior via rules and law—above all other concerns. This led, in many cases, not just to survival but also to the thriving, economically and politically, of the most morally organized group.

Stage 3: The Economy-Driven Family. Human economics, which dominate today's families, were far less sophisticated when our religious texts were written. This has changed, especially in the last two thousand years. While the fight for survival is always basic, agriculture helped more and more people survive to old age. While the need for moral law is basic to humanity, that need was, for the most part, satisfied by the sacred texts of each culture (and each family's baseline adherence to the authority of those texts) during the era of morality-driven families.

But humanity is constantly flowering. Having dealt with basic survival and morality, the human being moved toward creative innovation. Those of us born in the last hundred years especially benefit from this movement. Adults in our civilization judge their effectiveness as human individuals by their ability to reach *economic* goals—moral life is relative. Economics are the human currency that allow for constant innovation, direct human competition to worthy goals, and, in the main, feed families.

In the United States or Japan, we can certainly see survival-driven families—mainly among people below the poverty level—as well as morality-driven families—mainly among the very religious. But we see, in most cases, economy-driven families: families surviving and being ethical while mainly being driven by the stimulation of economic goals, issues, ideas, and technologies.

In the United States and Japan, two relatively homogeneous societies, we don't see all three evolutionary stages of the family still alive equally in the way I did in India. In India, because there are fifteen official languages, countless different tribes and groups, high population and countless gradations of poverty and wealth, homogeneity is less possible, economic foundations are less firm, and the support of extended families is a more obvious daily necessity for all citizens. *Most people can't survive without extended family help.* The extended family provides not only economic bases, but also moral teaching.

When I lived in Hyderabad during my boyhood, I lived in these circumstances, but as a child, I was not developed enough to understand it. In the 1980s, when I lived and taught in Ankara, Turkey, I saw many of the same components as I studied extended-family systems in rural Turkey. It was in Turkey that I looked back at the United States and at India, and understood that extended family is more crucial to all the stages of family development than had been realized. Returning from Turkey, I discovered the neural sciences we've discussed in this book. I also discovered that they all hint to what some sociobiologists come right out and say: "Tribal and family groups ensure the best health for the human child." Human ethologist Phon Hudkins has put it plainly: "The healthiest way to raise human children is through a tribe." Our popular culture has recently—though too superficially—embraced this basic idea in the saying "It takes a village to raise a child." The science of sociobiology prefers to look even more deeply into the concept, a concept that human religion has, as we've noticed in all of our chapters so far, hoped to support.

There is a very rich form of family available to us, one in which science and religion meet. In it, nature and nurture are one. Parents and others—grandparents, teachers, neighbors, mentors, friends—care for the *whole child,* the *soul* of the child, and they are entranced by the child. In this family, the child is holy, not only a survivor (survival driven) or a citizen to mold (morality driven) or an economic protégé of human money-making institutions, but a living breathing soul, the flame at the center, the source of human love. This kind of family knows the child as the completion of life.

Stage 4: The Soul-Driven Family. This is the kind of family system that has taken care of basic survival, provided for moral and economic needs, and now longs for the deepest possible connection with the inherent energy of the universe. I saw inklings of this family in India, in Turkey, in Japan—indeed, it is everywhere. And certainly it emerges here, in the United States.

This soul-driven family cannot be successful without the *extended family,* the tribe. The last thirty years have proven to us that harried and time-crunched nuclear and single-parent families cannot succeed to the highest levels of effectiveness, nor provide the deepest quality of care for the child, unless they are helped and supported.

As we all probably intuit, living out our very busy, stimulating, immensely stressful daily lives, our civilization has not reached a point where the economy-driven family has succeeded in providing for us the soulful life we all, inherently, seek—a life in which we feel complete, whole, and in sync with our natural and divine intentions. But we may well also intuit that we are getting closer to our goals. We have, in every generation, become economically stronger; we have made our moral dialogues more sophisticated; and huge majorities of many world cultures are thriving rather than simply surviving. Now it is possible for the soul-driven family to be the family of the future. Knowing the details of the soul-driven family can help us grow toward it more fully.

THE FAMILY OF THE FUTURE

How can we recognize and effectively create a soul-driven family? The first step is to realize that attachment is primary. In a soul-driven family, a child is encircled by attachments. The family does whatever it takes for the primary caregiver, at birth and during infancy, to be able to keep the child nearby. But the family does more too. The encirclement of attachments protects adolescence too, with mentors everywhere. The soul of the adolescent is abandoned in our economy-driven culture, and families of the future will watch this time of life very carefully.

In all areas of attachment, the extended family may include

grandmothers, aunties, grandfathers, uncles from the child's blood relations; but it also may include "nonblood relations"—day care workers, nannies. It is slightly more difficult for nonblood relations to raise other people's children, but it is also one of the greatest challenges of our human future. For instance, there are times when one's own parents live far away or are too mentally ill to be of great use as caregivers to one's children. In these cases, nonblood relations—the communities we form in which to raise children—become more important. Throughout everyday life, nonblood relations attach to our children, and it is partly the work of parents to make sure that healthy nonblood relations are an intricate part of the care of the child.

Beyond basic attachment throughout the stages of soul growth, we will further know we have achieved a soul-driven family—and a civilization that supports it—when these things are accomplished:

1. Human attachment and bonding become a primary component of *corporate* culture. *No corporation of any size should consider itself a corporation of integrity unless it makes corporate day care available.*

   In the late 1990s, Lisa Brown, a state representative in Washington, was pilloried for breast-feeding her infant son on the floor of the Washington State legislature. From the economy-driven point of view, her activity "got in the way of business." But from the soul-driven point of view, her activity was actually quite courageous (and she did it with all due modesty). She was challenging government corporate culture to be child- and soul-driven.

2. Every child will receive a deep sense of ancestral lineage. Much of this must be passed on by elders in the extended family (and this is just as important for adopted as biological children). Geneologies will become germane to child rearing. Children will get to know better their soul markers.

3. The nuclear family (including single-parent or blended families) will open itself to extended family members, and extended family members will remember that quite often the nuclear family—especially the child's mother and father—need the extended family to adjust to *them,* not vice versa. Extended family members will approach schools, faith communities, and other institutions, making sure that these institutions are accountable for the child's welfare. It is nearly impossible for only the mother, or for a mother and father who are both working, to fully protect and advocate for the light of the child.

4. The media, which is now a significant part of a child's soul development, will be better controlled in a soul-driven family than an economy-driven family. Nuclear and extended family together will spend so much time with children that televisions and Gameboys in a child's room, or unsupervised Internet access for children under sixteen, will not be necessary for child development, and will only superficially be yearned for by the child. The soul of the child, in other words, will be so well stimulated by more natural lights, that the artificial lights become less needed.

5. Where mother and father are unable to help the child enjoy many hours in nature, the extended family will make sure the child receives the care of nature. In a soul-driven family, nature is foundational, and children will be guided to learn what dwells in their minds already from millions of years of hunting and gathering—the rhythms, sounds, smells, stimulations, and harmonies of the natural world. The light of nature—the photosynthesis, electromagnetic storms, and tingling mysteries, which are the soul's nutrition—will never be separated for too long from the growing light of the child.

6. A child's emotional and moral development will *both* be considered primary in a soul-driven family. One will not dominate the other. If a nuclear family seems especially obsessed with one, the extended family helps provide balance with the other. If a father, for instance, is rigid in his moral rules and provides little emotional support, the mother and extended family might support rules but provide more emotional nurturing. If a mother provides, perhaps, immense amounts of emotional support but has difficulty providing discipline, the extended family, again, will fill in the gap.

When many people care for the child, all share in the responsibility and all share any blame. The limitations of one caregiver are not felt so deeply by the child, and by others. The encircling family and community make sure that all limitations become strengths, and all strengths are equalized. As soul-driven families direct the child's light, they do it as a unified whole.

7. Parents will be encouraged to retrieve soul and be provided constant support when doing so. They will, thus, become better parents. To the extent adults have not retrieved soul, the child will be protected from them by the buffer of the extended family. When there is only one caregiver, there is greater chance that the dark spots on the soul of an adult will make for darker lives in the children.

   The Swiss psychologist Alice Miller said, "If you had a good childhood, give your children the childhood you had. If you had a bad childhood, give your children the childhood you always wanted." It is a simple rule, but one much harder to follow without the support of many caregivers who buffer children from damaged adults and who make it possible, by their care of the child, for adults to take the time to retrieve soul.

8. Marriage will be protected, not to the cost of the soul of either party, but for the soul of the child. Keeping a marriage strong will be considered not only the duty of husband and wife, but also part of the obligation of the extended family. Marital privacy is certainly important, but not when someone close to a child sees that one party in a marriage is creating harm to that marriage and child. If we are destroying our marriage, then each of us needs to have the courage to hear people we love tell us so. And each of us, as extended-family members bonded with a family and child, needs to have the courage to intervene, as politely and firmly as needed, in the lives of those we love. If the child is the light of our lives, the parents' marriage is the wax in the candle.

9. In the soul-driven family, that which is living will, in general, be more important than that which is virtual. Gail, my wife, once said: "What's important? Not movies or material things, but our friends, family, our pets. The trees in the backyard. The leaves. What's *living* is important." In nearly all religions a distinction is made between the material world and the hidden world of light—between reality and illusion. We all intuit that what carries the greater and more complex electrical pulse is more important to us. We have an intuitive knowledge of where soul is—in what people—and where it resides—in what places. It resides more completely in that which is more electrochemically alive and alert—the living, not the virtual.

When God is fully the child for all of us, the soul-driven family will become the norm. In the future of each of our families—if not in the present—is the challenge to see the child as God, as soul; and from this seeing, to wonder what God needs of each of us. I hope you will find, as I have, that God needs these things we've just explored.

WHEN GOD IS THE CHILD

"Give a little love to a child, and you get a great deal back." With these words the nineteenth-century English writer John Ruskin begged his society to deal with its own issues of character regarding how it treated children. At that time, child labor was a major issue. In our time, our children experience their own kind of mistreatment—their often unrequited need for constant, healthy human attachment. British anthropologist Ashley Montagu has summed up what we have learned in this book: "The child who has not been loved is biochemically, physiologically, and psychologically very different from the one who has been loved." We might be able to go even further and say, "The way God is loved in our homes and communities alters God in these homes and communities."

In the end we are saying that the soul of the child depends on us to realize that *God needs us.* The universe, we have thought, works because God answered *our* prayers. It is possible now to see, through the lens of science and religion, that the universe works because we, through care for the soul of the child, have the profound responsibility, and joy, to answer the prayers of God.

When God is the child, there will be less loneliness for children. We think of our children as kids; what if we thought of them as souls? With this idea, we began the substance of this book. As this book progressed, we wondered even further: What if we thought of our children not only as kids, or as soul, but also as *God?* How would this change human life?

I hope I have helped you to think of children that way. When I was growing up, under a great deal of family stress, it was a salvation for me to visualize myself as an individual separate from my family. I ran away from home many times—I separated myself. Once fully separate, I realized what a lost soul I was and worked for decades to retrieve the soul I had lost.

Initially, my separation was key—my individualization was key—but throughout my process of soul retrieval, and then upon becoming a husband and parent, I realized how many other people, throughout my childhood and young adulthood, gave me life. Many people (and even my parents, throughout their difficulties) saw the God in me. These were people who had the courage to help me push beyond my quest for separate individuality and find the ways in which I was completely connected to *all life.*

MOVING BEYOND INDIVIDUALISM

"We must be willing," wrote E. M. Forster, "to let go of the life we have planned, so we can have the life that is waiting for us." Those of us looking for new options for family and human life are now challenged to let go of some of the life planned by our economy-driven family—its pull toward disconnection and overstimulation—in order to discover the soulfulness available to us. One thing we might let go of is the almost obsessively individualistic lives we lead. We might realize that our economy-driven families, for all their gifts, pull us into an almost obsessive individualism, cut us off from full human life, make us lonely. If you have suffered a great deal of soul stress in your family of origin, this economy-driven impetus is even more disfiguring to your soul. Individualization is an important part of the process by which soul flowers. But individualism is another thing entirely—it is the belief that "I have to do it alone." When I hear clients speak this language, I hear their loneliness. While there are times in life when one must separate oneself from a person or persons who are dangerous, there is never a right time in life to believe that one must be lonely in order to survive.

So say the new sciences of the human mind that we've explored together, but not yet the culture of individualism we live in. We are a very individualistic society of adults—one that teaches children to "need nothing from anyone." This idea is a convenience in an economy-driven culture, which creates a competitive society of adults that runs counter to the sense of connectedness that the soul of the child instinctively feels for all of life. By nature, children are merged and meshed together. Young children, especially, know very little about "boundaries." Individualism does not reflect the soul of the child but the discernible ideas of adults who see people primarily as individual, discrete, and separate economic units. But children are webbed together among themselves and among the adults who care for them. And their brains need the webbing.

The obsession with individualism in recent human development has been a great blessing but has, to a great extent, confounded our human spiritual intuitions, which yearn to see all light as One Light.

The new sciences show us how to see individuality and connectivity seamlessly. The wisdom hidden in these sciences is useful as we plan to combat loneliness.

In a thousand years, we will probably be much better at overriding individualism with innovations like telepathy. Every generation is using a little more of the human brain, and perhaps one day we will override obsessive individuality in our mental processing. We will, thus, as adults, accomplish what the soul of the child already (simply by living the life process) accomplishes: union. We will live the unified field, the sense of being one with the light we are, on a daily, even moment-by-moment, basis.

Until then, however, our course is one of vigilance, and the children around us provide us not only the reason to be vigilant but also the pure sense of life itself from whose well we can drink.

The children in the synagogue suspected that they were God. I hope, now, as you come to the end of this book, you suspect it too. How beautifully balanced life can be when we really see the unity of all life that is before us and courageously embrace it.

*　　　*　　　*

The soul of the child can now be proven to humanity. The growth of the soul can be both observed and directed. The markings of God on the soul have become clearer. The physics of the light of the soul can be connected, now, to the light in all things. The soul's journey of growth in a lifetime can be observed and guided, both in its darkness and its light. And the children themselves have become so intelligent, they can make known to us their humanity even when they feel that the needs of God are not being met in their times of loneliness.

If I have learned anything from my own experiences and from other children, it is the following simple fact I now accept and hope I have been able to prove to you: God is my children, and God is yours. With this fact in mind I continue forward in my life, hoping that I can live a life of care, compassion, and vision like Great-grandma Laura, now ninety-six, has lived.

EPILOGUE

For those who have come to grow, the whole world
is a garden.

—BAWA MUHAIYADDEEN

To Great-grandma Laura, nothing mattered more than her children, grandchildren, and great-grandchildren. When in her old age her soul began its journey of separation from her body, she remembered her life as a sequence of moments with children. Her primary focus—beyond trying to protect her everyday health—was the soul of the child. Not only did this focus keep her a little younger, a little more vibrant every day, but it also gave her incontrovertible proof that her life had meant something significant to the world.

As you move forward in your life, I hope you will use the soul of the child as your starting point. I hope you will determine the meaning and morality of everything you do by how your actions affect the child. With the kind of new science, religious understanding, and vision available now, I hope you are now able to rethink childhood, the care of children, and human life.

We are poised at the edge of new possibilities. The growth of the human mind is making it possible for us to provide our children with the gifts of human freedom. Each person and family that makes a commitment to rethink childhood is committing to everyone and every child the great secret of human existence: We can always do better for our children than previous generations have done.

This keeps us going. This makes all our work worthwhile.

A guru from India, Gurumayi Chidvilasananda, was asked to describe devotion. She answered: "It is very important that your devotion includes everybody. 'God' does not mean somebody living up in heaven; God is the light which exists in everyone's heart."

The Book of Samuel reads: "Man looks at the outward appearance, but the Lord looks at the light within the heart."

And so it is that we come full circle to the light that our children are, to the hidden treasure of the child. May we never let anything in life take us away from that light. There is no light more important, and it is not an exaggeration to say that the light of the child is the best mirror of who we are, not only as individuals, but also as a civilization.

NOTES AND REFERENCES

PART I: THE SOUL OF THE CHILD

Silent Fire by James Connor (Crown, 2002)

CHAPTER 1:
THE SCIENCE OF THE SOUL:
PROOF OF THE SOUL'S EXISTENCE

Infinity in Your Hand by William Harper Houff (Skinner House, 2000)

SPECT stands for single photon emission computed tomography. PET stands for positron-emission tomography.

Seeing the Light

Religious Texts and Commentaries include:

The King James Bible.

The Bhagavad Gita, translated by A. C. Bhaktivedanta Swami Prabhupada (Bhaktivedanta Book Trust, 1972).

The Teachings of the Compassionate Buddha, edited by E. A. Burtt (New American Library, 1955).

Awakening the Buddha Within by Lama Surya Das (Ballantine, 1997).

The Traditional Jewish Siddur (prayer book).

Kabbalah by Perle Epstein (Shambhala, 1988).

Purgatorio by Dante, translated by John Ciardi (New American Library, 1957).

The Confessions of St. Augustine, translated by John K. Ryan (Doubleday, 1960).

The Meaning of the Glorious Koran, translated by Mohammed Marmaduke Pickthall (New American Library, 1974).

The Illuminated Prayer by Coleman Barks and Michael Green, (Ballantine, 2000).

The Prophet by Kahlil Gibran (Knopf, 1994).

"From the Heart of the Andes" by Hal Zina Bennett, *Shaman's Drum*, Fall 1994, 44-46.

The Science of the Soul

The High House by James Stoddard (Warner, 1998), p. 130.

"The Power of Light" by Joel Aschenbach, *National Geographic,* October 2001.

Information about sound and the body can be discovered in *Meditation as Medicine*, Dharma Singh Khalsa, M.D., and Cameron Stauth (Pocket, 2001).

CHAPTER 2:
THE SOUL GROWS: SOUL DEVELOPMENT FROM BIRTH TO ADULTHOOD

Tagore paraphrased from Deepak Chopra's *How to Know God* (Harmony, 2000).

Watch the Light Grow

Sources for world religion quotes include:

Oneness by Jeffrey Moses (Ballantine, 1989).

Infinity in Your Hand by William Harper Houff (Skinner House, 2000).

The Perennial Philosophy by Aldous Huxley (Harper, 1944).

The Secret Life of a Child

Lijun Wang's work is reported by Joel Aschenbach, "The Power of the Light," *National Geographic,* October 2001.

The Human Journey of Individualization

Sigmund Freud is quoted in *The Light around the Body* by Robert Bly (Harper & Row, 1967).

Stage 1: The First Three Years of Life

Contributions from a Decade of the Brain to Infant Mental Health, edited by Allan Schore. "Attachment Relationship on Right Brain Development," *Infant Mental Health Journal* (Jan.–Apr. 2001)

"Your Child's Brain" by Sharon Begley, *Newsweek,* February 19, 1996.

Stage 2: Later Childhood

For references to children and nutrition, see *The Biology of Success* by Robert Arnot (Little Brown, 2000) and "Unhealthy Habits" by Claudia Kalb, *Newsweek,* May 8, 2000.

Flowering

The *Infant Mental Health Journal,* edited by Allan Schore (vol. 22,

Jan.–Apr. 2000) is an immensely valuable study of how attachment stress alters brain growth. Fogel and Blanco are quoted from "Attachment Relationship on Right Brain Development."

A Culture of Cortisol

For Daniel Amen's work, see, among others, his book *Healing the Hardware of the Soul* (Free Press, 2002).

In Over Our Heads by Robert Kegan (Harvard University Press, 1994).

A Cure for Cortisol—The Extended Family

The Wonder of Girls by Michael Gurian (Pocket, 2002).

CHAPTER 3:
SOUL MARKINGS:
THE DIVINE MAP A CHILD IS BORN WITH

The Alchemist by Paulo Coelho (Harper San Francisco, 1993).

Genetics: Soul Markings

I learned of the Kohainim study from Rabbi Jack Isakson, Temple Beth Shalom, Spokane, Washington.

"Genome: The Race to Decode the Human Body" by Geoffrey Cowley and Anne Underwood, *Newsweek* April 10, 2000.

"New Twin Studies" by Nancy L. Segal, *Psychology Today,* September/October 1999.

Does Your Child Have a Destiny?

Laurie Beth Jones's book, *The Path,* is quoted in the Reverend Clare Austen's article, "Your Mission or Your Life," *Discoveries,* November 2001.

What Is Evil?

"The Genetic and Psychophysiological Basis of Antisocial Behavior" by Adrian Raine and Jennifer J. Dunkin, *Journal of Counseling and Development*, July/August 1990.

"The Roots of Evil" by Sharon Begley, *Newsweek*, May 21, 2001.

A Fine Young Man by Michael Gurian (Tarcher/Putnam, 1998).

Violence and the Peace Rock

Astrid Lindgren's story is quoted in the International Peace Exchange Newsletter, December 1999.

What Is Death?

The Eagle's Quest by Fred Alan Wolf (Touchstone, 1991).

PART II: GOD IS THE CHILD

Audre Lorde is quoted from *Cries of the Spirit,* edited by Marilyn Sewell (Beacon Press, 1991).

CHAPTER 4:
THE NEW HUMAN:
HOW OUR THINKING MUST CHANGE

Information on Albert Einstein was garnered from the following sources:

Ancient Light by Alan Lightman (Harvard University Press, 1991).

Subtle Is the Lord—The Science and Life of Albert Einstein (Oxford University Press, 1982).

"The Private Albert Einstein" by Peter Bucky (Andrews and McMeel, 1992). Reprinted in *The World Book Encyclopedia,* 1999.

Cultural Geographer I. G. Simmons is quoted in *The Humanizing Brain,* James B. Ashbrook and Carol Rausch Albright (Pilgrim Press, 1997).

God Is a Verb by Rabbi David Cooper (Riverhead, 1997).

St. Augustine is quoted from *St. Augustine's Confessions,* translated by Henry Chadwick (Oxford University Press, 1991).

Unitheism

I am indebted to the Reverend William Harper Houff and his book *Infinity in Your Hand* (Skinner House, 2001) for many of the unitheism quotes. See the chapter on "The Perennial Philosophy."

Two other books have greatly helped:

The Essential Mystics by Andrew Harvey (HarperCollins, 1996).

History of Mysticism by S. Abhayananda (Atma Books, 1994).

Aldous Huxley's *The Perennial Philosophy* is still a masterpiece in this tradition (Harper, 1945).

Dean Inge is quoted from *The Platonic Tradition in English Religious Thought* (MacMillan, 1926).

CHAPTER 5:
SOUL RETRIEVAL:
THE PERSONAL JOURNEY BACK TO THE SOUL

The opening quote is from *The Humanizing Brain* by James B. Ashbrook and Carol Rausch Albright (Pilgrim Press, 1997).

The Science of Lost Soul

Daniel Amen is quoted from *Firestorms in the Brain* (Mind Works Press, 1998).

The Science of Soul Retrieval

Why God Won't Go Away by Andrew Newberg, Eugene D'Aquili, and Vince Rause (Ballantine, 2000).

The Upanishads are quoted by Andrew Newberg, et al.

The New Human: Putting Children First

Teach Your Children Well by Madelyn Swift, (Childright, 2001).

Brad Pitt was quoted in *The Spokesman Review,* Nov. 24, 2001.

CHAPTER 6:

GOD IS THE CHILD:
THE FUTURE OF THE FAMILY

I received the Mother Teresa quote via E-mail from a reader.

God Needs Us

"The Wonder Beyond All Hope: The Life of Symeon the New Theologian" by Marilyn Gustin, *Darshan Magazine,* 1991.

Wendell Berry is quoted in the *UU World,* January 2002.

Alta is quoted in *Cries of the Spirit,* edited by Marilyn Sewell (Beacon Press, 1991).

The Loneliness of the Child

"Giving of Yourself to Others Can Cure Loneliness" by Judi Light Hopson, Emma Hopson, and Ted Hagen, *Knight Ridder/Tribune,* July 30, 2000.

"Anatomy of Melancholy" by Andrew Solomon, *The New Yorker,* January 18, 1998.

"Kids Need Protection from Market Exploitation" by John Kafensiz, *The Spokesman Review,* May 15, 2000.

"Use of Antidepression Medicine for Young Patients Has Soared" by Barbara Strauch, *The New York Times,* August 10, 1997.

"Are We Overdosing Innocent Children?" Fern Christenson, *The Spokesman Review,* February 28, 2000.

"More Adults in U.S. Corrections System" by Jennifer Loven, Associated Press, August 27, 2001.

The Good Son by Michael Gurian (Tarcher/Putnam, 1999).

"Incidence of Major Depressive Disorder and Dysthymia in Young Adolescents" by CZ Garrison, et al., *Journal of American Academy of Child Adolescent Psychiatry,* April 1997.

Sociobiology researcher Phon Hudkins is the founder of the Human Ethology Institute in Washington, D.C.

EPILOGUE

The Bawa quote can be found in *The Illuminated Prayer,* Coleman Barks and Michael Green (Ballantine, 2000).

Gurumayi is quoted in *Darshan* Magazine, August 1992.

BOOKS THAT HELP
NURTURE
THE SOUL OF THE CHILD

The following list is only a partial representation of recent books that advance the vision and concepts we have explored together. In compiling the list, I have not included ancient sacred texts, such as the Bible, the Koran, the Upanishads, or the Lotus Sutras. Nor is this list exhaustive; it is meant only to be a beginning.

THE SCIENCE OF THE SOUL

Why God Won't Go Away by Andrew Newberg and Eugene d'Aquili (New York: Ballantine Books, 2001). This book provides a very accessible guide to the newest research linking the brain with the search for God.

How to Know God by Deepak Chopra (New York: Three Rivers Press, 2000). Quantum physics provides the basis for this passionate exploration of the behind-the-scenes reality of the divine.

Zen and the Brain by James Austin (Cambridge: MIT Press, 1998). This is a highly academic approach to the science of the soul. Though difficult for some to read, it is perhaps the most detailed book in existence on the subject.

THE NEW HUMAN

The Seat of the Soul by Gary Zukav (New York: Simon & Schuster, 1999). Few books have popularized man's search for the new human better than this insightful look at what late-twentieth-century thinkers know about soul.

Infinity in Your Hand by William Harper Houff (Boston: Skinner House, 2000). With the phrase from William Blake as its title and starting place, this very readable volume, filled with references to every world religion, reveals an elder minister's personal understanding of the perennial philosophy and the new kind of humanity this philosophy describes.

Anatomy of the Spirit by Caroline Myss (New York: Harmony Books, 1996). Using the Hindu seven chakras as its foundation, this powerful book is a guide to the journey toward the new human that every individual can potentially make.

SPIRITUAL PARENTING

The Spiritual Life of Children by Robert Coles (Boston: Houghton Mifflin Co., 1990). An insightful look, by a renowned Harvard psychologist, at what "spiritual life" really means when used in the context of families and children.

Raising Spiritual Children in a Material World by Phil Catalfo (New York: Berkley Publishing Group, 1997). The spiritual life of children is very difficult to ensure in a world that seems almost set up to oppose it. This book is a primer on how to ensure it, against all odds.

Ten Principles of Spiritual Parenting by Mimi Doe (New York: HarperPerennial Library, 1998). Part inspiration, part practical tips, this book is a gentle companion for parents and mentors interested in basing their parenting on the premise of God and soul.

SOUL MARKINGS

Soul Prints by Marc Gafni (New York: Pocket Books, 2001). Based on a Jewish perspective but branching out into numerous approaches to our spiritual link to the past, this book is very well written and often joyful to read; it displays the soul right before our eyes with numerous commonplace, and quite mysterious, markers.

The Soul's Code by James Hillman (New York: Warner Books, 1996). Few spiritual writers of the late twentieth century match James Hillman for intellect and wisdom. In this book he puts his mind to answering questions about what it means to think of ourselves as completely (genetically) linked to the divine.

Cries of the Spirit, edited by Marilyn Sewell (Boston: Houghton Mifflin Co., 2000). This anthology of women's writings did not set out to show how embedded in the soul are universal themes from the genetic past, but this beautiful anthology reveals it in every word.

SOUL RETRIEVAL

Meditation as Medicine by Dharma Singh Khalsa and Cameron Stauth (New York: Pocket Books, 2001). This book is both soul-based and science-based, and that is its brilliance. It deals with the field of "medical meditation," combining spirituality and medicine to help individuals and a collective society heal.

The Miracle of Mindfulness by Thich Nhat Hanh (Boston: Beacon Press, 1975). Perhaps one of the clearest manuals in print on how to retrieve soul in everyday life, this slim book speaks very loudly.

Care of the Soul by Thomas Moore (New York: HarperCollins, 1992). Few guidebooks to spiritual maturity and healing have been more influential than this one. Moore, a former monk, brings forward the medieval traditions of soul care to help guide out present world toward a new sense of life and joy.

THE FUTURE OF RELIGION

Ethics for the New Millennium by His Holiness the Dalai Lama (New York: Riverhead, 1999). Along with *The Art of Happiness* and *How to Practice,* this book provides readers with the wisdom of a social thinker who writes about compassion with courage and heart. The Dalai Lama has the ability to write as both a monotheist and a unitheist, making him one of those progressive religious minds who never forgets that wisdom is only as useful as it is practical.

Original Blessing by Matthew Fox (Bernalillo: Bear & Co., 1983). This is one of the many books by the former Catholic priest who has become internationally recognized for his "Creation Theology." Bridging the worlds between monotheism and unitheism, Fox shows the other side of Original Sin—the blessing.

Son of Man by Andrew Harvey (New York: Tarcher/Putnam, 1998). This retelling of the life and philosophy of Jesus Christ from a unitheistic perspective begins with one of the most beautiful lyrical expressions of the human condition written in the English language.

ABOUT THE AUTHOR

Michael Gurian is a passionate advocate for children and families. A social philosopher, family therapist, and best-selling author of fifteen books, he is the cofounder of the Gurian Institute, which conducts research, launches pilot programs, and trains professionals. As a social philosopher, he has pioneered efforts to bring neurobiology and brain research into homes, schools, and public policy. A number of his groundbreaking books, including *The Wonder of Boys* and *The Wonder of Girls,* have sparked national debate. Translated into over a dozen foreign languages, his work reflects the diverse cultures (European, Asian, Middle Eastern, and American) in which he has lived, worked, and studied. He and his work have been featured in *The New York Times, USA Today, Newsweek, Time,* and on the *Today* show, *Good Morning America,* PBS, and National Public Radio. He lives in Spokane, Washington, with his wife, Gail, a family therapist, and their two children.

Michael Gurian can be reached on the worldwide web at www.michaelgurian.com.

INDEX

abandonment of the family, father's, 139, 160
aboriginal peoples, 31, 33, 77, 179
abuse, 61, 65, 97, 98, 102, 139, 173
Achenbach, Joel, 19
addictions, 57, 162, 180
adolescence, 57–58, 99–100, 191
   hormones in, 56, 57
   soul retrieval in, 158
   suicide in, 182
adopted children, 193
adrenaline, 152
advertising, 183
aerobic exercise, 158–59
affect synchrony, 62
after-death experiences, 106–07
aggression, 62, 82
Albright, Carol Rausch, 145
alcohol:
   alcoholism, 147, 154
   drinking during pregnancy, 139
al-Hallaj, Husein, 133
Alta (poet), 176
"Amazing Grace," 149, 152, 155, 161

Amen, Daniel, 63, 150–51
amygdala, 62
Anatomy of the Spirit (Myss), 212
ancestral lineage, awareness of, 193
"angels," 142
Anne Frank Principle, 66
anorexia, 64
antidepressants, 153, 154
antisocial personality disorders, 95, 103
Aquinas, Saint Thomas, 17
Aristotle, 17, 22
artificial intelligence, 123
Ashbrook, James, 145
astrophysicists, 43
atheism, 159
athletic problems, 56
attachment, 39–41, 59–60, 97, 99, 124, 136, 140, 158, 166, 181, 197
   brain development and, 50–51, 52, 62
   destiny and, 92–94
   disorder, 164
   with mate, 160

attachment *(cont.)*
    multiple caregivers and, 66–67
    physical effects of lack of, 60,
        61–64, 99
    in soul-driven family, 191–92
attention deficit disorder, 66, 182
attention deficit hyperactive disorder,
    64, 66, 182
Augustine, Saint, 12–13, 17–18, 58,
    108, 130
aura, 25
Auschwitz, 159
Austin, James, 211
awwal, 14
Ayurveda, 76–77

bad thoughts, cingulate gyrus and, 96
behavioral problems, 56, 127
Bernard, Saint, 133
Berry, Wendell, 175
Bhagavad Gita, xviii, 10, 131, 138,
    188
Bible, 43
biological clock, light and, 19
birthing process, 3–7
    the monitors, 5–7
birthright, 77, 81
Blake, William, 3
blind, the, 28
"blood-brain" barrier, 83, 84
blood pressure, 60
body, the:
    -brain systems, 24, 26
    exterior of, 25
body and soul, unity of, 7, 10, 26–27,
    32–35, 43–44, 137–39
    importance to understand, for the
        care of our children, 139–41
    previous belief of separateness of
        body and soul, 21, 33, 138
body heat, 25, 27, 28
borderline personality disorder, 62
Brahman, 149
brain:
    adult growth, 58, 152
    attachment and development of,
        50–51, 52

"blood-brain" barrier, 83, 84
-body systems, 24, 26
brain stem, 23
cingulate gyrus, 96, 98, 99, 151
electromagnetic current running
    through the, 23
genetic programming and the, 82,
    83
hippocampus, 107
limbic system, *see* limbic system
major areas of, 22–23
moving toward greater use of, 123
myelination of cells of, 57–58, 59
neocortex, 23, 51–52
neural sources of the feeling of
    unity, 129–30
occipital lobe, 23
parietal lobe, 23, 107, 156
percent of the brain we use, 108
prefrontal cortex, 57, 96, 98, 99,
    107
pruning process, 55–56, 59
rewiring by violence, 98, 163
stages of child development and,
    see development of the soul
templated development, 59, 61
temporal lobes, 23, 96, 98, 99,
    107, 129, 156
trauma's effect on, *see* stress;
    trauma
breast cancer gene, 73
breathing, 31
Brinkley, Dannion, 106
Buddha, 10–11, 134
Buddhism, 111, 135
    development of the soul in, 42, 58
    soul as light in, 10–11, 108
    unity of body and soul in, 32
    Zen, 132, 134
bullying behavior, 100
Bundy, Ted, 163–64

Cabalists, Jewish, 11–12, 80, 122,
    132
Capra, Fritjof, 135
carbohydrates, 56
Cardoveros, Moses, 132

Care of the Soul (Moore), 214
caring for children, 128, 140–41
  putting children first, 165–68
  see also extended family; family;
    parenting
Catalfo, Phil, 212
Catherine of Siena, Saint, 133
cells:
  cellular activity, 22, 98
  copy of the genome in each of the,
    81
Chandogya Upanishad, 175
Character Regression Syndrome, 99
Chidvilasananda, Gurumayi, 202
children:
  attachment, *see* attachment
  caring for, *see* caring for children
  destiny of, 84–94
  development of the soul, *see* devel-
    opment of the soul
  divine map of, *see* soul markings
  divinity of, 76–79, 140
  future of, 139–43
  God equated with, *see* God, as the
    child
  loneliness of, 179–84, 197
  long-distance relationships with,
    93
  parenting, *see* parenting
  providing a safe world for, 126
  putting them first, 165–68
  raised in spiritual path, 127
  returning to the innocence of,
    157–58
  seen as economic interns, 181
  thinking of, as souls, xxi
cholesterol, blood, 60
Chopra, Deepak, 211
Chosen, The (Potok), 171
Christianity, xvii, 33, 58, 78, 127,
    129
  creation in, 31
  development of the soul in, 42
  evangelical, 122–23
  the Fall, 130, 131, 136
  Gnostic, 132, 133
  Jesus story, 169–72

mysticism, 133
  soul as light in, 12–13
Chuang-Tsu, 134
cingulate gyrus, 96, 98, 99, 151
cloning, 73–74, 83–84, 124
Coelho, Paulo, 69
Coles, Robert, 212
Collins, Francis, 85
Columbus, Christopher, 86
communication technologies, light
    and, 20
complex cell activity, 22
Confessions (Augustine), 12–13
conformism, 185
Confucius, writings of, 188
Connor, James A., 104
Cooper, Rabbi David, 122
corporations:
  advertising of, 183
  corporate culture supporting soul-
    driven family, 192
cortisol, 60–65, 98, 99, 150, 152,
    158, 181
Council of Economic Advisors, 184
creation, 19, 31, 43, 67
Cries of the Spirit (Sewell), 213

Dahmer, Jeffrey, 97
Dalai Lama, 214
Dante, 12
d'Aquili, Dr. Eugene, 155, 156, 159,
    201
David, King, 78
Davies, Paul, 75, 176
day care, 192
death, 103, 104–12, 132
  absence of electrical energy, 21,
    31–32
  immortality, 108–12
  minimum of electrical activity
    maintained after clinical,
    105–09
  soul markings continuing in prog-
    eny, 104
de Broglie, Louis Victor, 134
Declaration of Independence, 79
democracy, 79, 185

depression, 29, 64, 82, 98, 145–48, 154, 180, 182
  studies of, 184
Descartes, René, 18
destiny, 84–94
  attachment and, 92–94
  to care for children, 166
  guiding a child's, 86–92
  inborn predilections and tendencies, 86, 88
development of the soul, 39–68
  flowering, 58–59, 64
  individualization, stages of, 46–49
  protecting the, 65–67
  science of, 50–58
  soul-driven family, 194
  stage 1: first three years of life, 50–52, 99
  stage 2: later childhood, 52–56, 99
  stage 3: adolescence, 57–58
  stress, and cortisol, 60, 61–63
devil, the, 102–03
Dharmapada, 10–11
diet, 54, 56
dieting, 56
divine child, 76–79
divine right of kings, 79
divinity of children, 76–79, 140
divorce, 66, 98
DNA, 72–73, 82, 83
  testing, 85
  see also genetics; human genome
Doe, Mimi, 212–13
dyslexia, 64

Eagle's Quest, The (Wolf), 110
Eastwood, Clint, 28
eating disorders, 56, 98, 182
Eckhart, Meister, 133
economy-driven family, 188–90, 191, 192, 198–99
Eddington, Sir Arthur Stanley, 134
Edward, John, 108, 142
EEGs, 100
egalitarianism, 79, 185
Einstein, Albert, 20, 115–20, 125, 128, 134, 142

free invention and, 116
  on light, 20, 117
  unified field theory, 117–18, 125, 129, 135
electromagnetic energy, 29
  after death, 105–09
  birthing monitors reading, 6
  cloning and, 73–74
  death and absence of, 21
  of exterior of the body, 25–26
  as indestructible, 111
  life and, 20–21
  love and feeling of, 29
  PET scans reading, *see* PET scans
  unified field theory and, 118
  see also light
Emerson, Ralph Waldo, 134
emotional incest, 97
emotions and hormones, 57
energy and matter, equivalence of, 117, 136
Enlightenment, 79
Ethics for the Millennium (Dalai Lama), 214
evangelism, 122–23
evil, 94–103
  defined, 95
  depiction of, 102–03
  eyes of evil people, 27–28, 97
  factors aggravating the proclivity to, 97–100, 103
  genetic proclivity toward, 95
  irretrievable souls, 162–65
evolutionary biology, 187
exercise, 158–59, *see* physical activity
extended family, 64, 66–67, 184, 193
  as essential to soul-driven family, 190–91, 193, 194, 195
  in India, 186, 189
  violence in, 97
eyes:
  affect synchrony and eye contract, 62–63
  "cold," 27–28
  of evil people, 27–28, 97
  light in a child's, xx, 27

family:
  economy-driven, 188–90, 191,
      192, 198–99
  extended, *see* extended family
  four stages of the, 187–91
  future of the, xxvi
  morality-driven, 187–88
  soul-driven, 190–96
  survival-driven, 187
  violence in the, 97, 99, 137, 180
  see also caring for children; parent-
      ing
fats, dietary, 56
Fine Young Man, A (Gurian), 98
Firestorms in the Brain (Amen),
      150–51
flatlining, 107
flowering of the soul, 58–60, 64
Forster, E. M., 198
foster care, 164
Fox, Matthew, 214
Freud, Sigmund, 45, 47, 148, 165

Gafni, Marc, 213
Garvey, Mike, 110, 111, 141
gender:
  crime and, 98
  genetics, and behavior, 83
geneologies, 193
Genesis, Book of, 129
genetic engineering, 73
genetics, 72–76, 79, 80–84, 126, 178
  cloning, 73–74, 83–84, 124
  human genome, *see* human
      genome
  soul markings, *see* soul markings
"ghosts," 141–42
Gibran, Khalil, 15, 34–35
Gilder, George, 20
Gnostic Christianity, 132, 133
God:
  as above and separate from man,
      129, 130–31, 135–36, 179
  as the child, xxiii, xxv, 67, 112,
      142, 168, 172–74, 196–98,
      199, 200
  as light, *see* light

  mankind's need for, 174–75
  need for mankind, 175–79, 197
  as one with man, 8, 111–12, 137
  reunification with, 129, 130, 131
  unitheism, 126, 131–36, 161
Goddess religions, 33
  soul as light in, 15
God Is a Verb (Cooper), 122
grandparents, 140, 190, 192
  see also extended family
Grant, Sally, 163–64
Gurian, Davita, xviii–xxi, 173
Gurian, Gabrielle, xviii–xxi
  birth of, 3–7, 35–36, 173
Gurian, Gail, xvii, xx, 26, 196
  birth of Gabrielle, 3–7, 35–36
Gurian, Michael:
  background of, xxii, 171, 172,
      186, 189–90, 197
  epiphany, xviii, xx

Háfiz, 13
haloed exterior of the body, 25, 26
Harvard University, 182
Harvey, Andrew, 214
Haseltine, William, 81
Hasidism, 132
heart rate levels, 97, 98, 158
Heisenberg, Werner, 134
Heraclitus, 100
heritability, 96
  see also genetics; soul markings
heroes, 54
High Horse, The (Stoddard), 30
Hillman, James, 213
Hinduism, 58, 76–77, 131, 133, 134,
      138–39, 149, 161, 175
  body and soul as one in, 10, 32
  creation in, 30
  development of the soul in, 42
  nadis (energy channels), 31
  reincarnation, 111
  soul as light in, 10
  stages of individuality-develop-
      ment and chakras, 46–47
  Vedic, 132
hippocampus, 107

Hitler, Adolf, 97
holographs, 124
Holy Spirit, 13, 30
Homo infiniens, see new human
  (*Homo infiniens*)
hope, 162
Hopkins, Anthony, 28
hormones:
  in adolescence, 56, 57
  cortisol, *see* cortisol
Houff, Reverend William Harper, xv,
  134, 212
How We Know God (Chopra), 211
Hudkins, Phon, 181, 190
Huichol of ancient Mexico, 77
Human Ethology Institute, 181
human genome, 81–82
  disease-causing genes, discovery of,
    73, 85
  mapping of, 72, 73, 75, 80, 81,
    124
  original spark of the universe in
    everyone, 73
  soul markings and, 75, 80–84
hunter/gatherers, 187
hyperindividualization of children, 64

identity, individual, 186
imagination, 55
immortality, 108–12, 167
incarceration of young people, 182
Incas, 16–17
India, culture of, 185–86, 189, 190
individualization, 65, 67, 68, 197
  human genome and, 81
  hyperindividualization, 64
  moving beyond individualism,
    198–99
  stages of, 46–49
infancy to age three, development of
  the soul from, 50–52
Infinity in Your Hand (Houff), 212
infrared technology, 25, 115
Inge, Dean, 135
innocence, regaining of, 157–58
Inquisition, 133
Internet access, children's, 193

In the Line of Fire, 28
Islam, 33, 127, 129, 130
  creation in, 31
  development of the soul in, 42
  prayer cycle, 14
  soul as light in, 13–15
  Sufi, 132–33

James, William, 126
Japan:
  culture of, 185
  stages of the family in, 189, 190
Jeans, Sir James, 134
Jesus, 78, 102, 133
  story of the birth of, 169–72
Jones, Laurie Beth, 91
Jonesboro, Arkansas, school violence
  in, 99
Judaism, xvii, 33, 128–29, 171
  Cabala, *see* Cabala, Jewish
  creation in, 30, 31
  development of the soul in, 42
  genetic markers and, 80
  Kohain, Levites, and Israelites, 80
  mysticism, 122, 132
  soul as light in, 11–12, 108
judgment, prefrontal cortex and, 96
junk food, 56

kapha, 77
Kaplan, Louise, 60
karma, 111
Kegan, Robert, 64
Khalsa, Dharma Singh, 213
Kholberg, Lawrence, 48–49
Koran, xviii, 42, 130, 188
Krishna, 10
Kübler-Ross, Elisabeth, 106

language:
  genetics and, 73
  learning of, 59
LASER (light amplification by stimu-
    lated emission of radiation),
    20, 115
Lawrence, D. H., 105
learning problems, 56

light, 102, 135, 136
  ability to guide, 20
  cloning and, 73–74
  development of the soul, *see* devel-
    opment of the soul
  fusing of, 82
  immortality of, 108–12
  lacking volume, 19–20, 80
  lasers, *see* LASER (light amplifica-
    tion by stimulated emission
    of radiation)
  as material of the soul, xvii–xix,
    120
  molecules as, 74
  mood and, 30
  origins of the universe and, 19, 43,
    67, 75
  as particle, 20, 117
  philosophies of the soul and,
    17–18
  quanta, 117
  religions equating the soul, God,
    and, 9–17
  revealed when placed against a
    mass, 19–20
  slowed down by matter, 44
  soul markings and, 80
  sound and, 30–31
  speed of, 20, 22, 44, 136
  study of genetics, used in, 80–81
  as wave, 20
  see also electromagnetic energy
light coherence, 65
limbic system, 23, 29, 51, 52, 57, 62,
    99, 129, 152
Lindgren, Astrid, 101
Littleton, Colorado, school violence
    in, 99
loneliness, 30, 41, 64, 147, 179, 198
  of the child, 179–84, 197
long-distance relationships with your
    children, 93
longevity, 124
Lorde, Audre, 113
lost soul:
  defining the, 149–53
  science of, 148–53

Lotus Sutras, 42
love:
  child's need for, 102
  withholding of, 102
Lucifer, 102–03

Mahaparinibbana Suttanta, 10
Malkovich, John, 28
marriage, 195
Mary, Virgin, 78, 102
Masai tribe, 179
matter and energy, equivalence of,
    117, 136
maturity, psychological, 167
Maybury-Lewis, David, 85
Mead, Margaret, xiii
media, the:
  overstimulation of children by,
    183
  in soul-driven family, 193
meditation, 155, 156, 157, 158, 159,
    162
Meditation as Medicine (Khalsa and
    Stauth), 213
Me generation, 165
mental illness, 56, 65, 181
midlife crisis, 160
Millennium television series, 85
Miller, Alice, 195
Miracle of Mindfulness, The (Thich
    Nhat Hanh), 214
mission, helping a child articulate his,
    91–92
modeling behavior, 54–55
monological thinking, 34
monotheism, 126, 127, 128–31,
    135–36, 137
Montagu, Ashley, 197
mood disorders, 56
Moody, Harold, 106
Moore, Thomas, 214
moral development:
  stages of, 48–49
morality-driven family, 187–88
Moses and the burning bush, 11–12
MRIs, xxiv
Muhaiyaddeen, Bawa, 201

My Name Is Asher Lev (Potok), 171
Myss, Caroline, 212
mysticism, 134

Nachman, Rebbe, 11
nannies, 192
narcissism, 62, 103
National Human Genome Research
    Institute, 85
Native Americans, 16, 33
    touch healers, 25
nature:
    child's exposure to, 194
    man's relationship with, 175
nature therapy, 158
NEC Research Institute, 44
neglect, 97, 98, 99, 139
neocortex, 23, 51–52
nervous system, 24, 26
neurobiology, 178
neurons, 24
    child development and, 50, 51,
        58–59
    connections, 50, 53
neurophysics, 119, 125, 131, 136,
        178
neuropsychiatry, 153
neuropsychology, 148–53, 154,
        155–56, 157, 160, 165,
        167–68, 178
neuroreligion, 129–30
neurosciences, 20–21, 139
    death, understanding of, 105–12
    development of the soul evidenced
        by, 42–43
    electromagnetic energy and life,
        20–21
    exterior of the body and, 25–26
    unity of body and soul and, 32
    see also individual neurosciences
neurotransmitters, 22, 24, 154
Newberg, Andrew, 24, 154–55, 156,
        159, 211
new human (*Homo infiniens*), xxv,
        122–25
    polylogical thinking of, 34
New Testament, xviii, 188

nuclear family, 183–84, 186, 191
    openness to extended family, 193
    time crunch in, 184, 191
nutrition, 54, 56

obesity, *see* overweight children
oblivion, 105, 109, 111
occipital lobe of the brain, 23
Old Testament, xviii, 11, 128, 129,
        132, 136, 188
Original Blessing (Fox), 214
overstimulation, 64, 65
overweight children, 53–54

Paltrow, Gwyneth, 86
paq'o initiation among the Incas,
        16–17
paranoia, 103
parenting, 136
    attachment, *see* attachment
    care of children, *see* caring for
        children
    connection between parent and
        child, 167–68
    desire to feel meaningful as parent,
        121
    putting children first, 165–68
    societal support for, 140
parietal lobe of the brain, 23, 107,
        146
Path, The (Jones), 91
Pauli, Wolfgang, 134
"Peace Rock," 101
pedophilia, 162–63
Peggy, Grandma, xix–xx, xxvii
Pentecostal Christians, 30
personality disorders, 62, 95, 103
PET (positron-emission tomography)
        scans, xxiv, 115, 117, 119,
        120, 129, 149, 151, 162
    of children, 50, 51, 53, 54, 55, 61,
        62, 100
    electrical energy of our thoughts
        and actions, 20–21
    of evil people, 96
    of irretrievable souls, 163, 164,
        165

light indicating life, xviii, 26, 108
prayer and meditation's effect on,
  159
philosophical views of the soul,
  17–18
physical activity, 52, 53
Piaget, Jean, 47–48
Pitt, Brad, 166, 168
pitta, 77
Planck, Max, 134
Plato, 17
polylogical thinking, 34, 103, 111,
  141, 142
population growth, 78, 79, 187, 188
post-traumatic stress, 152
Potok, Chaim, 171
poverty, 61, 98
prayer, 156, 157, 159, 162, 197
  effective, 159
prefrontal cortex of the brain, 57, 96,
  98, 99, 107
Promise, The (Potok), 171
Prophet, The (Gibran), 514
prophets, religious, 78
prostitution, 182
Psalms, 132
psychics, 108–09, 110, 142
psychotherapy, 158
pulse rate, 97, 98
Purgatorio (Dante), 12
Pythagoras, 30–31

quantum physics, 139

racism, 61, 98
*Raising Spiritual Children in a
  Material World* (Catalfo),
  212
Ramachandran, V. S., 129–30
reading, 55, 59
recidivism, 162
reincarnation, 111
relational self, 160
religion:
  convergence of science and, xxii, 7,
    126–27, 135
  development of the soul, 42–43

future of, 126–37
light equated with the soul, 9–17
monotheism, 126, 127, 128–31,
  135–36, 137
primary reason for, 126
unitheism, 126, 131–36, 161, 167
see also *individual religions*
religious art, halos in, 26
role models, 54
Roman Catholicism:
  soul and light in, 13
Rumi, Jalal al-Din, 13, 14
Ruskin, John, 196

Samuel, Book of, 202
Satan, 102–03
Saul (later Saint Paul), 12
Schawlow, Arthur, 20
schizophrenia, 96
school violence, 99
Schore, Allan, 50, 62–63
Schrödinger, Erwin, 134
Schuler, Greg, 81
science of the soul, 19–35
  convergence of religion and, xxii,
    7, 126–27, 135
  electromagnetic energy, see electro-
    magnetic energy
  light, see light
  neurosciences, see neurosciences
Seat of the Soul, The (Zukav), 212
security, 61, 65
  lack of, 61
Seinfeld, Jerry, 86
self-confidence, 92
separation, 60
September 11, 2001, terrorist attacks
  of, 32
serotonin, 60
serotonin reuptake inhibitors (SSRIs),
  154
Sewell, Marilyn, 213
sexism, 61
sexual abuse, 61, 97, 147, 163
sexual addiction, 154
sexual exploitation of children, 182
sexual "heat," 27

shamanism, 15–17, 33, 160–61
  light in, 16–17
  soul markings and, 77
shaming, 97, 98
Shandara, 133
Shavante tribe of Brazil, 85
Sheldrake, Rupert, 29
Silence of the Lambs, 28
Simmons, I. G., 122
simple cell activity, 22
single parents, 66–67, 98, 191
skin conductivity tests, xxiv, 53, 97,
    100, 120
smoking, 140
social success, 185, 186
sociobiology, 181
sociopsychology, 167
Song of Songs, 132
Son of Man (Harvey), 214
soul, the:
  body and, as one, *see* body and
    soul, unity of
  development of, *see* development
    of the soul
  electromagnetic energy of, *see* elec-
    tromagnetic energy
  light as material of, *see* light
  lost soul, *see* lost soul
  philosophies of, 17–18
  proof of the existence of, 3–38
  religion and, *see* religion
  retrieval of, *see* soul retrieval
  science of the, *see* science
soul-driven family, 190–96
  key elements for achieving, 192–96
soul markings, 69–114, 126, 193
  death and, 104–12
  destiny and, 84–94
  divine child, 76–79
  evil, *see* evil
  human genome and, *see* human
    genome
  immortality of, 108–12
Soul Prints (Gafni), 213
soul retrieval, 153–62, 195, 197
  irretrievable souls, 162–65
  putting children first and, 165–66

support for, 195
techniques of, 154–62
Soul's Code, The (Hillman), 213
sound and light, 30–31
SPECT scans, 26, 96, 115, 124, 149,
    151, 155, 156, 159
Spielberg, Steven, 86
"spirits," 141–42
spirituality, 159
  biology and, 156
  spiritualization of society, 141
  spiritual maturity, 167
Spiritual Life of Children, The
    (Coles), 212
Stauth, Cameron, 213
Stefannson, Karl, 81
Stern, Daniel, 53
Stoddard, James, 30
stress, 183
  chronic, 97, 98
  cortisol levels and, 60–64, 98, 99,
    150, 152, 181
  post-traumatic, 152
Sufi Islam, 132–33
suicide, teen, 182
Sura III, 123, 130
Sura XVIII, The Cave, 13–14
survival-driven family, 187
Surya Das, Lama, 11
Sutras, xviii
Swift, Madelyn, 165
Sylwester, Robert, 64
Symeon the New Theologian,
    174–75

Tagore, Rabindranath, 39
Talmud, 138
Taoism, 134
Tao of Physics, The (Capra), 135
Tao Te Ching, 188
Teach Your Children (Swift), 165
telepathy, 199
television watching, 55, 193
temper control, temporal lobe and, 96
temporal lobe epilepsy, 129
temporal lobes of the brain, 23, 96,
    98, 99, 107, 129, 156

Ten Principles of Spiritual Parenting (Doe), 212–13
Theresa, Mother, 169
Thich Nhat Hanh, 214
thought disorders, socially destructive, 96
thyroid, 54
Tibetan Buddhism:
    soul as light in, 11
tobacco companies, 183
touch, sense of, 28–29
Townes, Charles, 20
trauma, 61, 152–53
    see also cortisol; stress
Turkey, 190
twins, studies of, 82–83, 95, 96

unified field theory, 117–21, 122, 125, 126, 127, 129, 135, 199
United States:
    homogenous culture of, 185
    stages of the family in, 189, 190
unitheism, 126, 131–36, 161, 167
University of Minnesota, twin studies, 82–83
Upanishads, 42, 161, 175

Van Praagh, James, 142
vatta, 77
Vedantists, 133–34

Vedic Hinduism, 132
violence, 97–98, 99–100, 102, 136, 180
    "Peace Rock" and, 101
    rewiring of the brain by, 98
Virgil, 12
vision, 51
vision quest, 160–61

Wang, Lijun, 44
Whitcher, Laura, xv–xvi, xx, xxi, xxvi–xxvii, 31, 173, 179–80, 201
Why God Won't Go Away (Newberg), 24, 154–55, 211
Wolf, Fred Alan, 110
Wonder of Girls, The (Gurian), 66, 98
Wordsworth, William, 157
work ethic, 185
World Health Organization, 182

Yezid, Abu, 132–33

Zen and the Brain (Austin), 211
Zen Buddhism, 132, 134
Zeus, 78
Zohar, the Book of Light, 12, 42, 132, 141
Zoroastrianism, 13, 108
Zukav, Gary, 212